The Complete Workbook for Science Fair Projects

The Complete Workbook for Science Fair Projects

Julianne Blair Bochinski

WILEY

John Wiley & Sons, Inc.

Published by John Wiley & Sons, Inc., Hoboken, New Jersey
Published simultaneously in Canada.

Design and production by Navta Associates, Inc.

For general information about our other products and services, please contact our Customer Care Department within the United States at (800) 762-2974, outside the United States at (317) 572-3993 or fax (317) 572-4002.

Wiley also publishes its books in a variety of electronic formats. Some content that appears in print may not be available in electronic books. For more information about Wiley products, visit our web site at www.wiley.com.

ISBN 0-471-27336-8

Printed in the United States of America

10 9 8 7 6 5 4 3 2 1

In memory of the grandparents I remember, Peter and Petronella Fallis, and the grandparents I wish I could have known, John and Ann Bochinski.

CONTENTS

ACKNOWLEDGMENTS

Once again, many thanks are due Science Service, Inc., for their advice and permission to reprint the official forms used for application to the Intel International Science and Engineering Fair. Thank you to Sister Mary Christine, assistant fair director and member of the board of directors of the Connecticut Science Fair. She is a former high school math department chairperson who has given many hours of her time mentoring and preparing students for science fair participation and competition for over thirty years, and I thank her for her insightful ideas and continued support of my books over the years. Acknowledgment is also due the Massachusetts State Science and Engineering Fair for their hospitality and good sense of humor in allowing me to stay to photograph and chat with their student contestants and judges after I caused them undue alarm with my clueless breach of security. I applaud you for your well organized event, dedicated committee members, and participants. Thanks for your kindness.

A very special thank you to the creative and talented student consultants who graciously provided their own personal stories for the case studies, namely: Christopher Waluk, Richard Grajewski, Brandon Habin, Colleen Muldoon, Sheela Chandrasheeker, and Lohith Kini. Your stories were amazing and inspirational. Finally, many thanks to my editor, Kate Bradford, for this opportunity; to my proofreader and friend, Rohan Goodsir, for his ideas and feedback in helping me finalize this workbook; and to my dear father and mother, Edmund and Elizabeth Bochinski, for always keeping me focused and motivated on this and many other projects.

INTRODUCTION

Over the past few years, I have visited a number of state and regional science fairs along with the grand event itself, the Intel International Science and Engineering Fair. The purpose of these visits was to research the latest trends and developments in the ever-growing and exciting world of science fairs for a new edition of my books, *The Complete Handbook of Science Fair Projects* and *More Award-Winning Science Fair Projects*.

While interviewing students, parents, and teachers, I asked them what they would like to see written about in a new book(s) about science fair projects. The response I received was rather surprising. While I imagined the majority would request award-winning science fair project recipes (okay, a lot of you did), there were actually a great number of requests for a simple, interactive science fair workbook that could be passed out by teachers to students in the classroom when administering a science fair project assignment, or by homeschoolers when introducing their children to the process of finding and completing a science fair project from scratch. These requests and suggestions came from a great deal of interest in treating the science fair project assignment as a separate course of study or class that would start at the outset of the academic year with a workbook of lessons, exercises, activities, and pages for students to take notes and write down ideas to help them through the assignment. Armed with those requests and ideas, I designed this easy-to-use interactive workbook that will take a student through the entire process of finding, completing, and submitting an award-winning science fair project of his or her very own. The workbook approach should help students make it to the top at their local science fair and get more out of the science fair process as a whole, rather than treat it as a burdensome homework project.

If you are brand new to the world of science fair projects or have a little experience and are ready to move forward with an interesting and exciting project, then this workbook is for you. Unlike science fair project "cookbooks" that offer you a selection of ready-made science fair project experiments to sample, this is an idea-generator workbook that will make you think like a student scientist (it really isn't painful at all!) and take you on your very own science fair project journey.

Through a series of fun and meaningful exercises, activities, and inspirational case studies, this interactive guide gives you the game plan of the steps and creative ways to find the right topic, formulate a meaningful hypothesis statement, focus on a project objective, develop an experimental plan, use statistics to analyze and present your data, write a project report, and get ready for oral presentation and judging. It takes you through all these stages of a science fair project in a short, methodical, and easy-to-use format that is suitable for any student in grades 5 through 12. A list of scientific supply companies, sample project journal worksheets, sample science fair project forms, and a notes section to record your thoughts and ideas are included in the appendixes.

For teachers and parents, here is a short interactive primer for your students and children to get them thinking on their own. You can choose the exercises and activities for them to work on or have them choose for themselves. For students, here is your coach with a game plan to help you through the entire science fair project process. Use it alone or in combination with the award-winning projects in *The Complete Handbook of Science Fair Projects* or *More Award-Winning Science Fair Projects* for more inspiration. Most importantly, use this book to focus on your personal interests and have fun with it! Today's world of science fairs and projects offers many exciting opportunities for achievement. I wish you great success.

1

SCIENCE FAIRS AND SCIENCE FAIR PROJECTS

THE GAME PLAN

To understand what a science project is and how it works. To understand what a science fair is and what happens at a science fair.

What Is a Science Fair Project?

A science fair project is different from any other type of project you work on at school. It is an independent educational activity that encompasses a variety of skills, many of which you have to teach yourself as you go along. A science fair project gives you hands-on experience and knowledge in your own independent field of study of a particular topic in science, math, or engineering. It is a challenging extracurricular assignment that allows you to use your own ideas to investigate a scientific problem or question that interests you according to a process called the **scientific method** (defined more fully in the box on the following page).

A science fair project is *not* a book report; a term paper; a history project; a collection; a demonstration of a well-known scientific fact, principle, or discovery made in the past; or a display of something in science or nature. Don't be confused by science projects that you may see in books or on the Internet that are designed specifically to demonstrate certain scientific principles. Those projects might provide instructions on how to build or construct various items, such as a windmill, a camera in a box, a battery, or an electromagnet or motor, or demonstrate how things like magnetism, air resistance or drag, or electrolysis work, and so on. Although those projects are wonderful to sample in your free time or as classroom projects, they are not the same as a science fair project. A true science fair project poses a specific scientific question, the subject of which is studied and tested in order to arrive at a credible answer or a better technique or final product. To give you an example, a science fair project usually presents a question, a problem, or a purpose in one of the following cause-and-effect formats:

> What is the effect of A on B?
>
> How does A affect B?

To demonstrate, just substitute A with one of the following terms:

- water content
- humidity
- temperature
- light

and substitute B with one of the following:

- bean plants
- earthworm behavior
- rusting
- heat conduction

Once you can identify a science fair project topic, you need to know how to work with that topic to scientifically answer the question that is being asked. Simply put, you use the scientific method, which is a way of thinking and approaching a science project topic.

THE SCIENTIFIC METHOD: THE BLUEPRINT

A **science project** may appear in many different forms, so it is helpful to understand the blueprint behind a science project: the scientific method. This method is a way to study a scientific problem in order to answer a proposed question or develop a better technique or final product through repeated tests and observations in a controlled environment. The scientific method consists of the following elements: problem or purpose, hypothesis, research and procedure, experiment, and analysis of results or conclusion. The following list defines each element of the scientific method and provides a basic example of how to work with a topic according to this method.

An Illustration of the Scientific Method

1. *Problem or purpose:* The question or **problem** you are seeking to solve.
   Example: Does listening to classical music influence memorization ability?

2. *Hypothesis:* Your observation or educated guess about what might take place through your research and experimentation, or your estimated solution to the problem and the results you expect to achieve from your experiment.
   Example: Since it is known that piano and singing instruction increases abstract reasoning skills in children (known as the Mozart effect), I believe that listening to classical music increases memorization ability.

3. *Research and procedure:* The process by which you gather information. This may include consulting reference materials and mentors or professionals in the scientific field you are studying, or other people or organizations related to your subject who will help you understand your topic. You will then use this information to formulate a procedure that will test your hypothesis through an experiment.
   Example: Through reading various articles and consulting with a professor of psychology at a local university, you may have learned about studies that have been conducted on the Mozart effect in terms of cognitive development. You may have learned about short-term improvement of spatial reasoning ability in human subjects that have been exposed to music by Mozart. Your **research** may have led you to wonder if memorization ability would also be improved by listening to Mozart's music.
   At this stage, you would try to develop an experimental plan to test or answer your

| continued |

query. You would need to identify what you are testing (for example, the ability of children to memorize) or the **dependent variable**—that aspect of the experiment that is being tested; how you will test it (for example, playing Mozart's *The Marriage of Figaro* while students memorize) or the **independent variable**—that aspect of the experiment that is being changed or manipulated; what controls will be used (for example, the ability of students to memorize without music) the **control** being that part of the experiment that is not altered or changed; and how the results will be observed and measured.

    Example: Two groups of seventh-grade students will be tested. Group I (the test group) will be asked to study the periodic table of the elements and the corresponding symbol for each element during a one-hour period while listening to the Mozart classic *The Marriage of Figaro*. Group II (the control group) will be asked to study the same material during a one-hour period of silence. At the end of one hour, each group will be given a written test to see how many elements they can recall when given the corresponding symbol for each.

4. *Experiment:* The process by which you carry out the procedure you outlined during the research and procedure stage to test your hypothesis. You will conduct tests using variables and controls and collect data results. An experiment is usually repeated several times to make sure consistent data results are obtained.

5. *Analysis and conclusions:* The stage where you analyze your data results in order to form a solution to your proposed question and proof or rejection of your hypothesis.

    Example: Based on the data obtained from this test, it appears that the introduction of classical music during study time does not have any effect in increasing memorization ability.

At this point, you will need to look at how the results may have varied among different students and trials. Are there ways that the experiment can be improved for future study of the problem?

    While a science fair project is modeled on the blueprint of the scientific method, which gives you the opportunity to think and work like a scientist, keep in mind that it also provides you with many more learning opportunities and skills. You will learn how to investigate; network (meet people and make connections); conduct interviews; follow rules and guidelines; use various scientific procedures, tools, and equipment; analyze **data**; draft an **abstract**; write a **report**; prepare a **display**; and speak in public, all in one assignment! Yes, a science project is a big assignment. However, when we break down this process into workable bite-size pieces, the task not only seems more manageable but becomes fun and rewarding. With work and dedication, the experience you will gain and the skills you will achieve from this extraordinary activity will reap you many rewards.

What Is a Science Fair?

Every spring, thousands of students in grades 5 through 12 prepare science fair projects for competitions held by school districts, regions, and states. These fairs are public exhibitions of the students' projects to recognize their work and to stimulate interest in science. Professionals from the scientific community often judge the science projects. Students who participate can earn valuable experience along with educational grants, scholarships, and other prizes. Additionally, many college recruiters give science fair project participation high marks in considering an application for college admission.

Most regional and state **science fairs** are affiliated with the **Intel International Science and Engineering Fair (ISEF)**. This prestigious science fair competition is held in May every year in a major U.S. city. The ISEF includes some twelve hundred top science fair projects from high school students around the globe who are winners from state and regional Intel ISEF–affiliated fairs. This annual event is administered by Science Service, Inc., a national nonprofit group based in Washington, D.C. Science Service also administers the **Discovery Channel Young Scientist Challenge** (for students in grades 5 through 8) and the very prestigious Intel Science Talent Search (for high school students).

If you would like more information about the Intel ISEF, the Intel Science Talent Search, the Discovery Channel Young Scientist Challenge, or an affiliated science fair in your area, contact

Science Service, Inc.
1719 N Street, N.W.
Washington, D.C. 20036
Phone: (202) 785-2255
Fax: (202) 785-1243
sciedu@scieserv.org
www.scieserv.org

— EXERCISES —

1. Look at the following project topics and determine which are science fair projects and which are not. What can be done with those topics that are not science fair projects to change them into workable science fair projects?

   - Does the design of an air glider affect its performance?
   - How radar works.
   - Do fat-free potato chips contain more oil than regular potato chips?
   - A study of the history and extinction of dinosaurs.
   - An examination of the types of seashells found off the New England coast.
   - Can a simulated volcano be built?
   - Does a correlation exist between aroma and the Mozart effect?
   - How does the human eye work?
   - What nutrient is best for cultivating yeast?
   - What method of water purification is most efficient?

2. Take the following basic project topics and determine the process for handling them using the scientific method. Think about how you would form a hypothesis statement, how and where you would research the topic, ways that you might develop a procedure for an experiment, and how you would collect your data. (You may need to conduct some minor preliminary research in order to work with the topics.)

Which antacid tablet will neutralize the most stomach acid?

Hypothesis:

_____

_____

Research and Procedure:

_____

_____

_____

_____

_____

_____

_____

Experiment:

_____

_____

_____

_____

_____

_____

_____

Analysis and Conclusions:

_____

_____

_____

_____

Does natural or artificial insulation work best?

Hypothesis:

_____

_____

Research and Procedure:

_____

_____

_____

_____

_____

Experiment:

_____

_____

_____

_____

Analysis and Conclusions:

_____

_____

_____

_____

At what pH level does bacteria grow best?

Hypothesis:

_____

_____

Research and Procedure:

_____

_____

_____

_____

_____

_____

Experiment:

_____

_____

_____

_____

Analysis and Conclusions:

_____

_____

_____

_____

2

FINDING A TOPIC: WORKING WITH YOUR INTERESTS

THE GAME PLAN

To find a science fair project that you are interested in and/or know something about.

Coming up with a great science fair project topic may seem like quite the challenge, but there are many ways to go about the process that are simple and fun. All that is required is a bit of creativity on your part. This chapter contains many ways for you to get on the path to creating your very own science fair project. Take your time and try the exercises and activities in this chapter. They will open your eyes to the many science project ideas you are actually surrounded with every day. This chapter will introduce you to several creative thought processes, so you are guaranteed to find a great project topic in a short period of time.

Before you start, remember that the key is to find a topic that you are interested in or know something about. Try to avoid a subject that is too general and try to think of a specific subject that interests you. If you need some examples, this chapter will show you how you can work a general topic into a specific one. Try the following exercise to see if you're already a pro at this.

— EXERCISE —

Each of the following topics may seem specific, but they are really too general because they can be developed in many different directions. See if you can narrow some of them into specific project topics. When you are done, flip to "The Subcategory List Approach" section of this chapter to see how we narrowed these general topics into specific ones.

1. What are the effects of stimuli on human memory?
2. Does food preservation affect mold growth?
3. What factors help seeds to germinate best?
4. What age-related factors affect night vision?
5. What effect do antioxidants have on the human body?
6. How can mold be identified and removed from homes?

7. Do natural mosquito repellents work?
8. Which antacid works best?
9. Can a computer program be written to find the best solution to a problem with multiple solutions?
10. What is the composition of river sediment?
11. What home insulation design is best?
12. What are the effects of worms on crops?
13. Can mathematical patterns be found in music?
14. What are the physics of a tennis racquet?

Your Interests, Experiences, and Resources

If you want to do a great job, you must choose something that you can get excited about. It's guaranteed to be reflected in your work. And remember that once you get started on your science project, you are going to have to live the life of a dedicated researcher on that subject for a couple of months or maybe longer. It's very hard to stay focused on a topic you don't really care about. With prior interest and enthusiasm about your topic, your project will take on a whole different meaning and you will be able to go the distance and do a great job.

KNOW THE CATEGORIES

Most state and regional science fairs have various divisions and categories under which all science fair projects are organized. Projects are first divided by age group. Contestants between grades 5 and 8 fall into the Junior Division of the fair, and students between grades 9 and 12 fall into the Senior Division. Within each Junior and Senior Division, you will find projects by individuals and teams (groups of two or three students). Within each division, every science fair project falls into one of two main categories. The **life sciences category** consists of projects that can be broken down into seven main subcategories: *behavioral and social sciences, biochemistry, botany, gerontology, medicine and health, microbiology, and zoology.* The **physical sciences category** consists of projects that can also be broken down into seven main subcategories: *chemistry, computer science, earth and space science, engineering, environmental science, mathematics, and physics.* Take a look at the following descriptions to get an idea of how these subcategories are defined and the key terms you will find when studying them. A sample of some of the procedures that are used is also provided. This will help you understand the techniques that scientists and researchers use within each main subcategory of science, many of which have also been used by award-winning science fair contestants over the years. Some of these methods might sound complicated now, but they'll become easier to understand once you get started on a particular topic.

Life Sciences

Behavioral and Social Sciences: The study of human and animal behavior and social science comprising anthropology, archaeology, biosocial determinants of behavior, child

| continued |

---

development, demography, development and learning, perception and learning, attention, memory, thinking, creativity, emotion, temperament, motivation, cognitive functions, processes of communication, language, aggression, family processes and social networks, attitude formation and change, ethnology, psychology, sociology, and so forth. Some procedures include behavioral observation, memory assessment, and statistical modeling.

Biochemistry: The study of the chemical and molecular basis of life processes comprising structure, chemical composition, organization and function of biomolecules, molecular cell biology, molecular genetics, proteins, nucleic acids, amino acids, lipids, enzymes, hormones, metabolism, recombinant DNA, RNA, molecular basis of disease, neurochemistry, blood chemistry, food chemistry, carbohydrates, polysaccharides, and so on. Some procedures include chromatography, electrophoresis, mass spectronomy, and protein sequencing.

Botany: A multidisciplinary field of study including biochemistry, medicine and health, microbiology, earth and space science, environmental science, physics and possibly other fields as they relate to the study of the life of plants, namely flowering plants, conifers, ferns, mosses and liverworts, algae, and fungi. This field encompasses the structure and reproduction of plant cells, agriculture, horticulture, plant taxonomy, forestry, plant pathology, hydroponics, plant genetics, plant hybrids, and processes of plant life including photosynthesis, respiration, plant environments, plant distribution, and so forth. Some procedures include germination and development of spores and seeds, tissue culture techniques, plant cell culturing techniques, plant electroporation and electrofusion, plant fertilization, cloning, and mapping population distributions of plants.

Gerontology: A multidisciplinary field of study including medicine and health, behavioral and social science, biochemistry, microbiology, engineering and possibly other fields as they relate to the aging process in living organisms. This area of study includes the psychology of aging, the life cycle of nutrition and metabolism, health issues, age-related disabilities, and devices for assisting the elderly. Procedures for this category vary and would correspond to the underlying multidisciplinary field of study used in a particular project.

Medicine and Health: A multidisciplinary field of study including behavioral and social sciences, biochemistry, microbiology, gerontology, engineering, and physics as they relate to the study of health and diseases in humans and animals. Pathology, pharmacology, all medical fields, nutrition, allergies, speech, hearing, and vision are part of this field. Procedures for this category vary and would correspond to the underlying multidisciplinary field of study used in a particular project.

Microbiology: A multidisciplinary field of study including biochemistry, medicine, health, and possibly other fields as they relate to the study of microscopic living organisms. Study areas include epidemiology and physiology of bacteria, viruses, fungi, protozoa, algae, pathology, antibiotic-resistant bacteria, eradication of infectious diseases, food microbiology, virology, immunology, microbial genetics, and industrial microbiology. Procedures for this category vary and would correspond to the underlying multidisciplinary field of study used in a particular project.

Zoology: A multidisciplinary field of study including behavioral and social science, biochemistry, medicine and health, microbiology and possibly other fields as they relate to

┤ continued ├

the study of animals, namely mammals, birds, fish, insects, amphibians, reptiles, and so on. This field comprises the physiology of animals, animal behavior patterns, animal habitats, animal genetics, processes of animal life, and so forth. Procedures for this category vary and would correspond to the underlying multidisciplinary field of study used in a particular project.

Physical Sciences

Chemistry: The study of properties and composition of matter comprising organic and inorganic chemistry, various forms of matter, reactions, and so on. Some procedures include reactions consisting of the change of liquids, solids, and gases, electrophoresis, chromatography, and oxidation-reduction.

Computer Science: The study of computer hardware, software, and various applications. Some procedures include working with artificial intelligence techniques, computer graphics, programming languages, modeling and simulation of biological or physical systems, design of computer hardware or software, encryption and coding, networking and communications.

Earth and Space Science: The study of the earth, its composition, and atmosphere and space comprising geology, geography, meteorology, astronomy, mineralogy, climatology, seismology, atmospheric physics, oceanography, marine geology, paleontology, and so forth. Procedures include identifying soil, water, air, and rock components, astronomical calculations, and weather prediction techniques.

Engineering: The study of constructing, designing, building, troubleshooting, or demonstrating a working model of a new product, a device to improve on an existing model or product, or an inventive model or device that solves an existing problem. This category includes projects that apply scientific principles to manufacturing and useful purposes in the areas of civil and mechanical engineering, heating and refrigeration, transportation, electrical applications, acoustical applications, and aeronautical applications. Procedures for engineering projects are often the subject of what is being studied.

Environmental Science: A multidisciplinary field of study of effects of natural and man-made changes on the natural world comprising ecology, pollution, vital issues affecting the natural world, sustaining natural resources, hydrology, limnology, hydrobiology, management of natural systems, and so on. Procedures for this category vary and would correspond to the underlying multidisciplinary field of study used in a particular project.

Mathematics: The study, development, and application of number theories and math principles comprising algebra, geometry, trigonometry, calculus, topology, algorithm analysis, and so forth. Procedures include solving and comparing mathematical proofs, verifying theorems, and developing a mathematical model to solve a problem.

Physics: The study and application of the physical properties, laws, and interactions of energy and matter comprising acoustics, light, thermal properties and insulation, optics, superconductivity, thermodynamics, magnetism, fluid and gas dynamics, and so on. Procedures include the use of optics, meters, lasers, circuits, transistors, amplifiers, regulators, spectroscopy, and electric and electronic devices and techniques.

The following techniques and exercises will assist you in focusing on how to work with the fourteen main subcategories in order to develop a possible project topic.

The Subcategory List Approach

The basic and most useful approach for finding a science project topic is to take the main subcategories of science listed above, combine them with your research of science news stories, your personal experiences, your personal resources or contacts with which you are familiar, and so on, and filter them down into second-, third-, and possibly even fourth-level subcategories of interest. These categories can then be distilled into possible project topics. With this approach, you create a list or hierarchy of categories and subcategories that stem from one of the fourteen main subcategories.

For example, say you are interested in and/or have a little knowledge about the main subcategory of *medicine and health*. As you think about this main-level subcategory, a second-level subcategory that might come to mind is *nutrition and diet*, then a third-level category might be *digestive problems resulting from chemicals in the body*. At this point you would think about what types of digestive problems would fall under this category and you might come up with something such as *lactose intolerance*. And if you chose *lactose intolerance*, you might narrow this sublevel category down to a particular aspect that you want to investigate. It might be a good idea to read and learn a little about lactose intolerance in order to develop some further categories. As you read up on this subject, you might learn that this digestive problem is caused by the human body's inability to digest a type of sugar found in milk and dairy products called *lactose*. Your initial research might lead you to wonder what could be added to the diet of a lactose-intolerant person to enable that person to digest milk products, and to the subject of *enzymes*, which might lead you to a possible scientific problem. For example, you might want to study *which type of enzyme hydrolyzes lactose best* or *what types of foods have the highest quantities of lactose-hydrolyzing enzymes*. A feasible project topic can be developed such as *a study and comparison of the quantity and potency of lactose-hydrolyzing enzymes found in various fruits*.

This approach really works well when you have no other starting point or when you want to narrow down broad ideas and subjects that you may come across through other brainstorming techniques. We are discussing this technique first and foremost because it allows you to collect your thoughts and information in an organized manner that will help you break down a broad category into a project topic. It is also one of the best techniques to turn to when you have many general ideas but are having trouble coming up with a specific topic.

The most important function of the list approach is that it allows your mind to wander through a variety of subcategories to see where you have some knowledge, interest, or available resources. Since you will find that you may have more ideas under one main subcategory than another, this method also provides a clear indication of the area of science that you should focus on for a project topic.

The List Approach Example

The following chart reproduces each of the fourteen main subcategories of the life and physical sciences and provides examples of how to use the list technique with each of the main subcategories to develop second- and third-level subcategories that can be broken down into possible science project topics. We have provided sample second- and third-level categories developed into actual project topics so that you can see how this process works.

Life Sciences

Behavioral and Social Sciences:

    Education and learning

        Study and memory techniques

            Effects of certain stimuli on human memory

Possible Topic 1: An investigation of the effect of color stimuli versus black and white stimuli on the learning rate of eighth-graders

Possible Topic 2: Do music, ocean waves, background TV, or silence enhance or detract from memory?

Biochemistry:

    Chemistry of food

        Food preservation and mold formation

            Growth rate of mold on different types of food

Possible Topic 1: Does the growth rate of mold differ between protein and carbohydrate foods?

Possible Topic 2: Which factor plays the most important role in preventing the growth of mold on food: temperature, carbon dioxide, or light?

Botany:

    Seed germination

        Factors that help seeds to germinate faster

            Effects of oxygen (light, temperature, water) on seed germination

Possible Topic: Do increasing oxygen concentrations enhance the germination rate of bean plant seeds?

Gerontology:

    Vision related to age

        Age-related factors affecting night vision

            Rate at which rhodopsin (chemical found in the eyes that is the key to night vision) forms related to age

Possible Topic: Does age affect the amount of time it takes for rhodopsin to form for night vision?

Medicine and Health:

    Antiaging nutrition

        Use and effects of various antioxidants

            Effects of polyphenols (a plant antioxidant found in tea) on free radicals (molecules or atoms with an unpaired number of electrons)

Possible Topic: How effective are tea polyphenols in reducing the damaging effects of free radicals?

| *continued* |

Microbiology:

Mold

Mold problems in homes

Means for identifying and removing mold from homes

Possible Topic 1: Which building material, if any, harbors the most mold spores?

Possible Topic 2: Which type of treatment works best in preventing the growth of mold on drywall?

Zoology:

Mosquitoes

Natural mosquito repellents

Natural stimuli that attract mosquitoes

Possible Topic: Analysis and comparison of the effectiveness of citronella oil, peppermint oil, and tea tree oil in repelling mosquitoes

Physical Sciences

Chemistry:

Over-the-counter remedies

Antacids

Effectiveness in neutralizing acid

Possible Topic: Which brand of antacid neutralizes the most acid at different titrations?

Computer Science:

Computer program for finding appropriate solutions to problems with many solutions

Simulated annealing algorithms (a method for finding optimum solutions by setting parameters to keep or discard various solutions)

Optimizing driving routes, traffic light patterns, and delivery schedules

Possible Topic: Configuration of optimal commuter driving routes using a simulated annealing algorithm

Earth and Space Science:

River sediment

Sediment composition

Sedimentation of sand, silt, and clay in the mouth of a river

Possible Topic: Does water salinity affect the rate at which clay settles and flocculates?

Engineering:

Modern home construction

Insulation designs

Materials used for insulation in modern home construction

Possible Topic: Which type of modern home insulation material works best?

| *continued* |

Environmental Science:

> Farming problems
>> Nematodes (worms that destroy crops)
>>> Environmentally safe methods for the eradication of nematodes
> Possible Topic: Can a crop-friendly fungus be applied to eradicate nematodes?

Mathematics:

> Math patterns
>> Math patterns found in music
>>> Common musical note transition patterns
> Possible Topic: Can the probability of rhythm and pitch transition patterns in music be calculated?

Physics:

> Physics in sports
>> Tennis racquet design and performance
>>> Tennis racquet string tension
> Possible Topic: Does the tension of the strings of a tennis racquet affect how quickly the strings will break?

In the following exercise, we have taken each of the fourteen main project subcategories as a starting point and provided you with three different secondary categories. From the fourteen main subcategories, choose five that you are most interested in and try to work at least one initial secondary category into a project topic. If none of our secondary-level categories interest you, create one yourself or use one provided by a teacher, friend, or parent.

— EXERCISE —

Life Sciences

Behavioral and Social Sciences

1. Subliminal learning

_____

_____

_____

2. Sensory perception

_____

_____

_____

3. Sociology differences among adolescents

_____

_____

_____

Biochemistry

1. Effects of vitamins and supplements

_____

_____

_____

2. Metabolism of carbohydrates, proteins, and fats

_____

_____

_____

3. Enzyme activity

_____

_____

_____

Botany

1. Gravity and plant growth

_____

_____

_____

2. Uses for algae

_____

_____

_____

3. Fruit rot elimination

_____

_____

_____

Gerontology

1. Metabolism in the elderly

_____

_____

_____

2. Changes in the five senses with age

_____

_____

_____

3. Devices to assist the elderly

_____

_____

_____

Medicine and Health

1. Evaluation of exercise programs

_____

_____

_____

2. Various physiological phases during active withdrawal from smoking

_____

_____

_____

3. Blood sugar and immune response

_____

_____

_____

Microbiology

1. Transfer of bacteria in beverages

_____

_____

_____

2. Antimicrobial effects of green tea

_____

_____

_____

3. Effects of antibacterial soap

_____

_____

_____

Zoology

1. Irradiated fruit and fruit flies

_____

_____

_____

2. Dog nose prints for identification purposes

_____

_____

_____

3. Diet modifications for health

_____

_____

_____

Physical Sciences

Chemistry

1. Causation and comparison of various chemical reactions

_____

_____

_____

2. Water purification techniques

_____

_____

_____

3. Rust formation and prevention methods

_____

_____

_____

Computer Science

1. Programming languages

_____

_____

_____

2. Modeling and simulation

_____

_____

_____

3. Computer graphics applications

_____

_____

_____

Earth and Space Science

1. Sand and soil erosion

_____

_____

_____

2. Solar power applications

_____

_____

_____

3. Effects of tides

_____

_____

_____

_____

Engineering

1. Bridge design evaluation

_____

_____

_____

2. Fin design and model rocket stability

_____

_____

_____

3. Insulation designs

_____

_____

_____

Environmental Science

1. Recycling and reclamation

_____

_____

_____

2. Air pollution control

_____

_____

_____

3. Eutrophication prevention

_____

_____

_____

Mathematics

1. Mathematical theorems

_____

_____

_____

2. Statistical modeling

_____

_____

_____

3. Mapping population distributions

_____

_____

_____

Physics

1. Force placement and center of gravity changes in martial arts

_____

_____

_____

2. Electromagnetic applications

_____

_____

_____

3. Power production

_____

_____

_____

Brainstorming: A Variation on the List Approach

A variation on the list approach is brainstorming, either on your own or with friends, parents, or teachers. You work in the same fashion as you did with the list approach. If you brainstorm with others, you will have the added benefit of their ideas.

Using the Main Subcategories to Brainstorm

Let's say that I pitch a main subcategory such as _environmental science_. You should respond with the first thing that comes to your mind. For example, let's say that you think of _effects on water quality_. In answering you back, I might throw out _public water plant purification_, and you might toss back _the quality of water in public schools_. I might respond with something that sounds more like a topic, such as _differences in the quality of drinking water among various public schools in the same water plant district_, then you might come up with another variation such as _does the distance that water travels from a water plant to various schools in the same district affect the amount of copper found in the water_.

See how easy that was? You can even perform this brainstorming exercise by yourself. Just start with a main-level subcategory and write down the first thing that comes to your mind. Follow with the next associated idea that comes to mind about this secondary-level category, and keep working down the list. Keep going until you cannot think of any more ideas. You might arrive at a great project topic!

To get an added benefit from your brainstorming session, try group brainstorming. As the old saying goes, two (or more) heads are better than one. If you brainstorm with a group in which everyone is looking for a science fair project, you can try the brainstorming technique using a variety of subjects, objects, or inventions as inspiration for the group. For example, your brainstorming group might have something as basic as a can of soda in front of them. You can actually work with that soda can in brainstorming ideas. Someone might make an observation about *the environmental impact of recycling aluminum cans*, someone else might toss out an observation about *the uptake of aluminum in the soda can beverage*, and yet another group member might make an observation about *the medicinal use of flat cola for treating an upset stomach*, and so on. Each of these observations could provide the basis for a great project topic. In general, the benefit of group brainstorming is that it will produce many ideas that can be worked into project topics for all the participants.

— Exercise —

Once you have a handle on how to brainstorm for science fair project topics, try getting a group of students, friends, or even family members together to assist you. The purpose of this exercise is to make as many observations as you can about a secondary-level category derived from one of the main-level categories. Challenge the group to come up with as many scientific observations as possible in a short period of time (say, ten minutes). You can even have the group make scientific observations about things in the room.

The goal is to be as open-minded as possible and record all possible suggestions. Don't discard an observation because it might seem ridiculous or funny. Keep the group momentum going and assume that the observations have a scientific counterpart from which a problem, purpose, or question can be developed into a project topic. When time is up, you should have a long list of observations. Some might be easily worked into actual project topics. But even if most of the observations made by the group are too broad, you can resort to the list approach, breaking them down into second- and third-level categories that may evolve into a project topic.

Your Experiences

Another way to select a project topic is to examine your past experiences. Have you ever had any experience that ties into a particular area of science? For example, perhaps you have brushed your teeth with a whitening toothpaste and wondered if there was a measurable difference between the results of your type of toothpaste and those produced by other over-the-counter whitening treatments. Perhaps you remember waiting a long time on an airport runway for the wings of your plane to be deiced for takeoff and wondering if the amount of time that it takes to remove the ice could be reduced through pretreating the wings with an oily substance. Or maybe you live near the coastline, where you have noticed a good deal of beach erosion in recent years and wondered what might be done to avert further erosion.

The following case study describes a successful science fair project that grew out of a student's personal experience.

PROJECT CASE STUDY #1: FINDING A PROJECT THROUGH A PAST EXPERIENCE
Bacterial Biofilms in Carpets, by Christopher Waluk

Finding a Science Project Topic "On the Floor"

Christopher Waluk came home from school with strep throat during the middle of winter, and it was not long before his younger brothers contacted the infectious bacteria from him. Two weeks later, just as Christopher appeared to have gotten over strep throat, he started to develop a sore throat all over again. In fact, this cycle repeated itself throughout the rest of the Waluk household as family members seemed to pass the bacteria back and forth. During this time, Christopher's mother sterilized everything in sight in an effort to stop one family member from transferring the bacteria to another; everything, that is, except the living room carpet.

The family eventually recovered from their bout with strep throat, but Christopher wondered if the living room carpet in his home had anything to do with spreading the bacteria. Since he and his brothers tracked through the carpet every day, carried food into the living room, and spent many hours sitting or lying on the carpet to read or watch television, Christopher found himself at the beginning of an intriguing scientific investigation that would spark four award-winning science fair projects on different phases of this idea.

Year 1: Designing the Initial Research Plan and Experiment

Christopher's goal with the first phase of his project was to examine various types of carpeting— from wool to plush nylon—in an effort to determine which one would retain the most bacteria after being washed with soap and water. Additionally, since many consumers treat their carpets with Scotchgard brand fabric protector, Christopher thought it might be interesting to expand his testing to see whether this substance would have any influence in inhibiting or encouraging the growth of bacteria.

After obtaining new carpet samples from a carpet retailer and sterilizing them in boiling water, he sprayed one-half of the samples with Scotchgard and left one-half of the samples untreated. He then obtained several common and harmless bacteria from a biological supply house and streaked them over the carpet samples. Christopher let all of these carpet samples stand for twelve hours. At the end of the twelve-hour period, he washed all the samples with soap and water and allowed them to dry.

In order to determine whether the bacteria remained in the carpets after being washed, he ran sterile applicators through each carpet sample and streaked them separately onto marked petri dishes. The results were shocking. Of all the carpet samples studied, the majority tested positive for bacterial growth after being cleaned. Additionally, some of the carpets that were treated with Scotchgard had heavier bacterial growth than their untreated counterparts. Christopher's work earned him finalist honors at the Connecticut Science Fair, which led Christopher to continue his investigation.

Year 2: Expanding the Initial Investigation

The second phase of Christopher's science project was to determine how long bacteria would stay viable in a carpet and what substances could be used to arrest their growth. Once again, he obtained new carpet samples from a carpet retailer and sterilized them in boiling water. He repeated the experiment by adding the same bacteria strains to the carpet. However, rather than wash the carpets after a twelve-hour period, he allowed the bacteria to stay in the

continued

continued

carpet samples and took cultures of all the samples every three days for a one-month period to determine how long the bacteria would remain viable in each of the different carpet sample types.

After finding that most of the bacteria remained viable for some time, Christopher decided to test typical store-brand carpet-cleaning products made specifically for shampooing and deodorizing carpets, along with a common household cleaning solution of white vinegar and water, to determine the effects each one might have on existing carpet bacteria. Christopher passed several sterile applicators across each of the carpet samples and streaked them onto separately marked petri dishes. He then soaked sterile filter paper disks in each of the cleaning solutions and placed them individually onto the streaked petri dishes. All dishes were incubated for a period of forty-eight hours, and the effects of the store-brand cleaning solutions were analyzed. The results were startling and showed that none of the carpet shampooing and deodorizing products inhibited the growth of bacteria in any of the carpet samples tested. However, the white vinegar and water solution did arrest most of the bacterial growth in the carpet samples.

At this point, Christopher decided to stop working with the carpet samples that were artificially impregnated with bacteria and take cultures directly from carpets in a multitude of homes in his town to determine if microbes other than the bacteria used in his initial studies were present. Under the guidance of a local lab technician, API and Catalase tests were performed on the cultures (tests that identify the types of bacteria present). Surprisingly, not only were all of the original bacteria strains initially studied found to be present in the samples but positive identification was made for pathogenic bacteria (bacteria that can cause infection or disease). Once again, Christopher's project earned him finalist honors at the state science fair along with the attention of area scientists, leading to an invitation to conduct more research at a corporate research and testing facility.

Year 3: Using Advanced Laboratory Techniques

The third phase of his project was to determine which carpet bacteria strain identified in Year 2 of the project dominated the others and in which carpet types. Once again, Christopher obtained new carpet samples from the carpet retailer as well as several pieces of new floor tile and oak wood flooring to serve as controls. He sterilized and inoculated each sample with the bacteria in various sequences and combinations utilizing the techniques he learned at the research center. After intensive research and testing through advanced methods, Christopher found that *Pseudomonas aeruginosa* outnumbered all other carpet bacteria.

Year 3 brought Christopher a place award at the science fair along with numerous awards and honors from special awards sponsors. Despite these achievements, Christopher still wanted to know about the nature of the carpet microbes he had studied, so Year 4—the final phase of his investigation—took form.

Year 4: More Advanced Laboratory Techniques

During one of Christopher's visits to the research center, he learned about biofilms, which are biological growths of microbial cells and extracellular polymers on a substratum that develop over a bacterium with time. In this last year of his project, Christopher's goal was to determine whether biofilms can establish themselves in carpet fibers, and if so, which types of carpet fibers are best suited for biofilms. Additionally, Christopher wanted to compare the different carpet bacterial combinations in the formation of biofilms and determine whether any carpets with natural fibers

continued

continued

have their own natural biocide that would inhibit or reduce the formation of a biofilm. Through advanced laboratory techniques, he found that biofilms were present on all of the synthetic fibers tested. However, of the natural fiber carpets, he found that only natural undyed wool did not provide an environment for biofilm formation.

The final year of this microbiological project earned Christopher one of the highest place awards at the Connecticut Science Fair as well as many awards and distinctions.

Science Project Insight from Christopher

Christopher's advice to students doing a science fair project for the first time is to look very

carefully at personal experiences for inspiration. Christopher developed an incredible science project from an experience that occurred right in his own family home. He also encourages students to keep pursuing their work for additional studies because it can be developed into possible future science fair projects if significant progress in the topic has been made since the previous year. For Christopher, his continued pursuit led to four related yet very distinctive projects.

Personal experiences provide a great foundation for secondary-level categories that can be broken down into workable science fair project topics. Need to jog your memory for personal experiences? Try the following exercise.

— Exercise —

Think of five things that you do every day while getting ready for school.

1. _____

2. _____

3. _____

4. _____

5. _____

Think of five places that you might have visited in the past year, either on a school field trip or a family trip, and write down one interesting or unusual quality or characteristic about each of these places.

1. _____

2. _____

3. _____

4. _____

5. _____

Name your five favorite foods and/or beverages.

1. _____

2. _____

3. _____

4. _____

5. _____

If you have pets, note the last time that one of them was ill, what the cause of the illness was, and how your pet recovered from it.

_____

_____

_____

_____

_____

_____

Name at least five major weather events that you might have experienced or witnessed in your lifetime. Note when, where, and why they occurred.

1. _____

2. _____

3. _____

4. _____

5. _____

Take one of the answers you gave for each question and develop a list of two, three, or more sublevel issues or categories in the following spaces. Try to work each of these into a possible project topic.

One of Five Things I Do to Get Ready for School Every Day

(Hint: A topic could be developed about the effectiveness of a common hygiene product or practice.)

Sublevel Issues:

_____

_____

_____

Possible Project Topic:

_____

_____

_____

One Interesting Thing about One Place out of Five That I Have Visited

(Hint: A topic could be developed about the environmental effects on a particular place you visited.)

Sublevel Issues:

_____

_____

_____

Possible Project Topic:

_____

_____

_____

My Favorite Food or Beverage

(Hint: A topic could be developed about the quality and nutritional benefits or deficiency of this food or beverage.)

Sublevel Issues:

_____

_____

_____

Possible Project Topic:

_____

_____

_____

The Last Time My Pet Was Ill Was Because . . .

(Hint: A topic could be developed about the cause, prevention, or treatment of this illness.)

Sublevel Issues:

_____

_____

_____

Possible Project Topic:

_____

_____

_____

A Major Weather Event I Experienced

(Hint: A topic could be developed about predicting this type of weather event, planning an effective way or building an effective device to withstand this type of weather event, etc.)

Sublevel Issues:

_____

_____

_____

Possible Project Topic:

_____

_____

_____

Innovative or Inventive Ideas You Have Had

As the old saying goes, necessity is the mother of invention. Another primary area for finding a topic is a close cousin to focusing on your past experiences. Have you ever developed a device or contraption to accomplish some purpose? Don't say no too quickly! Think about it. We have all been in situations that have led us to invent or create something to improve upon a product, a tool, or a system.

Need an example? Say your grandfather has a sailboat that is anchored in a mooring field and the only way to get to it is on an inflatable boat. Perhaps you remember a time when you and your grandfather went sailing and a storm suddenly developed that forced the two of you to get into the inflatable boat and head to shore. You might have felt uncomfortable with the wind and rain blowing on you as your inflatable boat motored into shore. You and your grandfather might have wished that the inflatable boat had a protective shield around it to protect the two of you from the elements. Once you got back to shore, perhaps the two of you began a lively discussion about a plan to build such a shield. Whether you and your grandfather actually built it is irrelevant. The point of this example is that a need developed from a problem, you identified the need, and you thought about a way to address it. If you had an idea like this, you might be able to turn it into a workable science project topic that might fit within the main sublevel category of engineering or physics.

— EXERCISE —

Think of a chore that you perform regularly. Have you ever imagined or actually developed a shortcut or technique to make the task easier? If not, can you think of something that can be done to make this job easier? Write down the idea and see if it falls under one of the main fourteen project subcategories. See if you can develop a project topic from this idea. (Hint: Perhaps you are in charge of taking out the garbage and sorting recyclable containers for your family. Have you developed a clever way to handle the removal and sorting of trash? Can this idea be developed on a larger scale for industry?)

Your Special Skills and Abilities

Think of a project topic in an area in which you have some skills or a related hobby. Perhaps you have sharp computer science skills or are a whiz at mathematical problem solving. Anything that you are good at or practice regularly can become the foundation for a terrific project. Skills and hobbies such as fishing, baseball, glass blowing, gymnastics, and even skateboarding all have certain aspects that can be turned into great science fair project topics. Even skateboarding? Absolutely! The physics of skateboard design, including centripetal force, momentum, gravity, and friction produced by skateboard bearings, could provide the basis for an excellent physical science project that might be fun and interesting.

The following case study describes an award-winning science project that was developed from one student's computer science skills.

PROJECT CASE STUDY #2: FINDING A PROJECT THROUGH YOUR SKILLS AND ABILITIES
A Line of Defense, by Richard Grajewski

Finding Inspiration through Scientific Abstracts
Richard Grajewski had always been interested in computer science. His older brother, Wally, was very talented in computer science and taught Richard many things about modeling and simulation. When science fair season arrived, Richard knew that he wanted to work with developing a complex computer model or simulation but was not sure what he could work with. Through the

continued

direction of his science teacher, he spent his free time researching the latest scientific abstracts on the Internet. He knew that he wanted to work on a topic of current interest and began to explore the popular main subcategory of medicine and health.

As he researched this main subcategory, Richard found many articles about viruses, which led him to many secondary-level subjects before he hit on something of great interest: the human immune system. With so many viruses and diseases in existence, from flu strains to more serious conditions, Richard saw a need to examine immune system response in greater detail. Most of the information he read on the subject indicated there were still many unknowns in this field. Much of the mystery seemed to center around problems in observing the immune system in action due to the microscopic size and detail of the mechanisms involved.

Richard became immersed in the current theories of how immune system response works. Through reading many articles and making contact with an immunologist who became a mentor, he began to ponder an alternative theory on the process. Before he even realized it, Richard was well on his way to reaching his goal: creating a complex computer model simulation with a real-world application.

Fascinating Research "Germinates" into a Science Project

Through many scientific abstracts, Richard learned that despite the great advances that have been made in the field of immunology, the immune system is still a great mystery to scientists. This may have to do with the difficulty in observing the immune system in action. The immune system is comprised of a selective process that is able to distinguish between foreign and host cells. The biggest responsibility of the immune system is to produce antibodies that will find an appropriate match to an antigen and therefore kill off the antigen. Richard learned that current theories say this is accomplished through a purely random search where antibodies roam the body and seek out matching antigens. When a contact is made, the antibody sends out two chemicals: one surrounds the antibody, which sends a message to B cells to produce more of the same antibody, and the second notifies a nearby cytotoxic T cell that it can engulf the bound antibody and antigen and remove them from the body.

Through many great discussions with his mentor, Richard became concerned that this theory seemed to overlook the element of time as an important detail in how all of this is achieved. Richard felt that finding a match randomly takes too much time and cannot be performed in the real world within a week (the average time span of the common cold antigen). After conducting much more research and continuing to consult with his mentor, Richard came to theorize that the immune system response process may not be random at all but rather organized in that the first chemical sent to the B cells is proportionately related to the connection strength of an antibody and antigen, and the second chemical is sent out only when an exact or very good match is made. Basically, Richard hypothesized that his proposed immune system theory would function in a way similar to what the current theory suggests, only faster. Richard built a simulated immune system computer model to test his theory and compared it to the current theory.

Building the Immune System Model

Using his research, Richard began to build his model, which was to be scaled to the real human immune system through ratios. The simulator worked on a 16-bit classifier system to represent the binding sites of the antibodies and antigens. Richard also included the three types of T cells, as well as B cells and their antibody-producing capabilities. Richard then performed experiments to determine the approximate number of generations it would take for a fixed number of

continued

continued

antibodies to find an exact match to one of four different antigens at the same time. He obtained data that identified kill frequency rates as well as the best mutation rates for quick binding site searches between antibodies and antigens. At the conclusion of his experiment, Richard's results showed that his theory was plausible and that antibody selection of antigens under his theory was much faster than the current theory. While actual real-world testing needs to be done to verify Richard's results, his work certainly accomplished all of his objectives and has paved the way for more research.

Science Project Insight from Richard

Richard received a prestigious third-place award among tough competition at the Connecticut Science Fair as well as first-place honors in the area of computer science. He encourages students to look closely at their skills and experience for inspiration. Richard says that even if you have a skill that is not technical in nature, take some time to examine it carefully. You might be surprised by its usefulness in developing a science fair project topic or in applying it toward your topic.

Tap into Your Personal Resources

While thinking about interests and past experiences, ask yourself who you can consult for a topic. Resources are everywhere. These individuals don't have to be teachers or scientists in order for you to tap into their background and find a great topic. One of the best and easiest places to start is right in your own home. Look at what your mom or dad does professionally. If your dad works as a car mechanic, he might be a great resource for a topic that investigates and compares antilock and lock brakes. If your mom is a dietitian, she might have some interesting insights for a project that examines the effects of food preparation on vitamin content. Don't forget other relatives, family friends, neighbors, your sports coach, your family doctor, the veterinarian, a plumber, your dentist, the landscaper, and so on. All of these individuals participate in careers that offer abundant ideas, resources, and connections for a project idea.

Write down the names of all the people with whom you interact on a regular basis. Under each of the names, list everything you know about the person's career, studies (if in school), hobbies, and outside interests. Then reread your notes and try to pick out key words under each person's name that might relate to one of the fourteen main subcategories. If some of these people have experience or expertise in one of the fourteen main subcategories, ask them if they will help you brainstorm and possibly conduct a science fair project in their particular field.

Sample List of Contacts

Name	Occupation	Special Skills	Hobbies
Mom	Pediatric nurse	Asthma specialist	Gardening
Dad	Home builder	Concrete specialist	Fishing
Uncle Bob	Airline pilot	Knowledge of airplane design, air tunnels	Sailing
My neighbor Mike	Church organist	Organ design, construction	All music
My sister, Sara	College student	Chemistry, pharmacology	Running/hiking

— EXERCISE —

Try to name at least ten people with whom you interact on a regular basis. Use the following chart to list their names and note each person's career field, special skills, and hobbies. Look over your list to determine if any of these people's careers are rooted in an area that can be broadly categorized under one of the fourteen main subcategories for science fair project topics or if any of their profiles indicate a connection to one of the fourteen main subcategories. Then contact one or several of the people to discuss the possibility of a science fair project in their area of specialization.

List of Contacts

	Name	Occupation	Special Skills	Hobbies	Main Subcategory
1.					
2.					
3.					
4.					
5.					
6.					
7.					
8.					
9.					
10.					

The following case study shows a great science fair project that was developed through a family contact.

PROJECT CASE STUDY #3: FINDING A PROJECT THROUGH YOUR PERSONAL RESOURCES
The Design and Application of a Tilt Rotor to a Tandem Helicopter, by Brandon Habin

Resource Contact for Idea
Brandon's grandfather, Henry Rettstadt, is a retired engineer from Piasecki Helicopter Corporation. Brandon's grandfather helped him to brainstorm the idea for his science fair project and turn it into a workable topic. Henry's experience with helicopter engineering and design also made him a great mentor.

An Idea "Takes Off"
While looking at the latest issue of a mechanics magazine, Brandon read a story about a project being performed at NASA to create a tilt rotor for a helicopter. He found the story fascinating,

continued

continued

since his grandfather had worked as a helicopter engineer. Brandon used the Internet to look for more information about this subject because he thought it would be interesting to design a device that would allow a helicopter rotor to tilt. Brandon was not able to find much on the subject except he learned that NASA was keeping its ongoing project secret. Excited about the concept, Brandon called his grandfather to discuss turning the idea into a science fair project. Brandon's grandfather was enthusiastic about the idea, too, and with his expert assistance as a mentor, Brandon embarked on his award-winning engineering science fair project.

An Engineering Project Takes Form

Brandon learned that the current configuration of a helicopter rotor poses problems in the steering mechanism. The steering system used in most helicopters changes the pitch of the blades on the main rotor at different intervals to destabilize the craft in a particular direction. NASA proposed a solution to this problem in the mid-1990s, suggesting that a variable tilt rotor, that is, one that could tilt in any direction while a helicopter is in flight—was the answer, since the tilt rotor would allow for a decrease in aerodynamic drag, noise production, vibration at speeds greater than 140 knots, and the amount of power needed to fly such a craft. It was found that a universal joint with a directional steering mechanism would allow for this tilt. Brandon proceeded to conduct more research and found that the most versatile universal joint was a ball-type constant velocity joint, which can take maximum load and stress.

Once Brandon finished his initial research, he arranged a time to meet with his grandfather to discuss how he could design the device that would allow a helicopter rotor to tilt. Luckily for Brandon, his grandfather had an entire machine shop in the basement of his house. He began his engineering project by constructing a complex ball joint. He accomplished this through drafting on paper a design that would allow for a helicopter rotor to tilt in any direction at a maximum of 30 degrees. He then incorporated his sketches into a computer drafting program called Auto Desk Inventor®, as well as Solid Works®, a program for designing parts and assemblies.

Through the help of his grandfather/mentor, the ball joint was designed to be driven by a pinion gear and supported by tapered roller bearings within a stationary unit. This concept design was only tested for functionality, not for stresses and durability. According to Brandon's computerized virtual model and the physical model he constructed, there were no clearance or binding problems. All of the parts were fully functional and allowed for the rotor mast assembly to tilt while rotating. Brandon was pleased to see that the completed physical assembly almost exactly matched the specifications of his drafts.

continued

continued

Science Project Insight from Brandon

After receiving finalist honors at the Massachusetts Science and Engineering Fair, Brandon went on to become a semifinalist in the Siemens Westinghouse Competition. Brandon emphasized that first-time science project students should attend a science fair exhibition to get a hands-on idea of what projects look like and what types of ideas other students have implemented. Additionally, Brandon highly recommends making contact with individuals who can assist in providing direction and advice. He indicates that while it is difficult to pick up the phone and make a cold call to a stranger for help, it is well worth the effort. In Brandon's case, a call and follow-up letter to a computer program company resulted in his receiving a complimentary copy of one of the software programs he used in the design and development of his tilt rotor prototype.

Scientific Abstracts, the Internet, Traditional Periodicals, Current Events, and Local Topics of Interest

Scientific Abstracts

Good sources for a science project topic are scientific abstracts. They are located in bound scientific journals that are usually available at a college or university library. These specialized journals are used primarily by science professionals. Articles are generally grouped into two classes: research experimental reports and reviews of scientific literature. If you don't have access to a college or university, you can find many scientific abstracts on the Internet. A key word search on Google.com for the words *science*, *abstract*, *research*, and *experiment* will reveal an abundance of abstracts that are accessible right from your computer. A variety of abstracts on topics from plant and soil science to physiological science to astronomy are widely available.

Some abstracts are highly technical articles and some are not. In either case, the best approach is to write down the key terms and science vocabulary words that you find in the article. Also, when you are finished reading the abstract, try to summarize what you read in your own words. Reread your notes, key terms, and scientific vocabulary words. All of this information can be worked into great secondary-level subcategories that you can break down into project topics through the list technique described earlier in this chapter.

The Internet and Electronic Periodicals and Magazines

There are many terrific Web sites and electronic periodicals available online that contain a wealth of information about many different areas of science. The vast number of science fair project–related Web sites makes it difficult to list the best sources for you to consult. However, the following Web sites are some favorites for generating a project topic as well as general science fair project information.

HELPFUL WEB SITES FOR SCIENCE PROJECT IDEAS

www.scienceproject.com/index.asp   One of the largest Web sites for science project ideas, information, and support.

www.scifair.org   Web site of the Society for Amateur Scientists. Contains ideas for projects, research, links, and more.

www.school.discovery.com/sciencefaircentral/index.html   The Discovery Channel's science fair resource guide. Contains information on completing a project and a guide for teachers.

www.sciencenews.org   A publication of Science Service that contains interesting and timely scientific articles.

www.sciencedaily.com   Contains links to the latest science research news from which science project ideas can be developed.

whyfiles.org   Contains a real-life approach to scientific news stories from which science project ideas can be developed.

www.isd77.k12.mn.us/resources/cf/welcome.html   Cyber Fair. Contains science projects and information for younger students.

www.exploratorium.org   Web site of the Exploratorium Museum. Contains project ideas and interesting science content.

www.spartechsoftware.com/reeko   Reeko's Mad Scientist Lab. Contains science project ideas and other interesting science project information.

www.sci-journal.org/index.php   *Sci-Journal* is an online publication for science students. The journal, based in England, gives students the chance to publish work they have done in their science class so that other science students can see it.

www.madsci.org   MadSci Network. This group of scientists can provide answers to your science project questions. A lot of interesting information as well.

Established Scientific Magazines with Great Web Sites

www.nationalgeographic.com   Web site of *National Geographic* magazine.

www.discover.com   Web site of *Discover* magazine.

www.popsci.com/popsci   Web site of *Popular Science* magazine.

www.scientificamerican.com   Web site of *Scientific American* magazine.

www.motherearthnews.com   Web site of *Mother Earth News* magazine.

www.popularmechanics.com   Web site of *Popular Mechanics* magazine.

— EXERCISES —

1. Write down the fourteen main subcategories and challenge yourself to find a different current event news story that can be categorized under each of the main subcategories. Write a summary of each news story under the applicable heading. Reread your summary and pick out the key terms and scientific vocabulary words in the article and try to work them into a project topic.

   For example, a news article on forest fires in the western United States might discuss fire-containment methods used by firefighters or perhaps the aftereffects of these methods on flora and fauna. This article would probably work well under the main subcategory of environmental sciences, where you could summarize the article into a project topic such as "What Are the Effects of Various Flame Retardants on Evergreen Trees?" or "Which Type of Flame Retardant Is Most Effective in Reducing the Flammability of an Evergreen Tree?"

2. Watch five news programs during a given week. Note every science-related story in the news and take notes on each story. Then go back and try to categorize each story under one of the fourteen main subcategories. See if you can break down a story into a workable science project topic.

   For example, a recent news story indicated that scientists have found that methane bubbles can dangerously erupt and rise to the surface of the sea from chunks of solid methane found on the seafloor. This may explain why some ships and vessels have mysteriously disappeared over the years. This story yields countless possibilities. The story could be categorized under the main subcategories of earth science, environmental science, physics, and even engineering. Under each of these main subcategories you could list a different aspect from the news story. Under earth science you could start with *effects of deposits of solid methane on the seafloor*. Under physics you could start with *the loss of buoyancy of a ship or vessel due to the presence of methane gas bubbles*. Under engineering you could try *the bubble-buoyant boat: redesigning a sailboat to withstand the trough of a methane gas bubble*. Under environmental science you could begin with *the environmental effects of methane gas bubbles on aquatic life*.

See how easy it is to hone in on a project topic when you organize your thoughts under the main project subcategories and work from there? With this approach you can easily see how one news story can be broken down into four different possible science project topics. This sure makes watching the news more interesting and exciting!

Current Topics of Interest

Many successful science fair project topics share a common theme: they tend to focus on a new technology, problem, issue of current interest, or a novel approach to an ongoing problem. Recently, many students have been fascinated by applications of new technologies, such as wireless communications; urban planning problems, such as noise reduction in major cities; microbiology, such as antibiotic-resistant bacteria; and environmental science, such as forest fire prevention and water/soil contamination studies. If you need inspiration for a topic on a current issue or technology, log on to America Online and type the key words *science, health,* and so on, and you will retrieve excerpts of many current news articles in various scientific subject areas. Also, while browsing America Online, be sure to check out the key words *science fair.* You will get helpful information on science fair projects, including a few message boards where you can interact with other students to get ideas or advice.

— EXERCISES —

1. Imagine that you found the following science news article while surfing the Internet. (This passage was taken from a real news story.) Read the article. In the space provided, write down all the key words and science vocabulary terms. Look up the definitions of science terms that you are not familiar with and write them next to the terms you selected from the article. Then try to summarize the article in about two sentences. Go back over your notes. In the space provided, create a list of all applicable science fair project main subcategories as well as all second- and third-level categories. Finally, try to develop a project topic from one of your ideas.

IRRADIATING MEAT CAUSES CONTROVERSY

Irradiation is sometimes used in the treatment of meat before it is sold to consumers in order to kill bacteria, insects, parasites, and other organisms to reduce the risk of unwanted disease such as salmonella and *Escherichia coli.* Irradiation is an electrical process whereby meat is treated with brief amounts of gamma rays or electron beams. While cooking meat to the "well-done" point will usually kill such organisms, the purpose of irradiation is to reduce the risk of disease when meat is eaten by consumers in an undercooked stage—that is, anything not "well done." Recent studies have shown, however, that irradiating meat may change the meat's chemical composition such that when it is consumed it may produce harmful by-products in the body, which may lead to unhealthy consequences and disease. These studies are preliminary, however, and further research is being conducted to determine the long-term effects of exposure to irradiated meat in one's diet.

Science Vocabulary Terms Found and Defined:

_____

_____

_____

_____

_____

_____

Summary of Article:

_____

_____

_____

_____

_____

_____

Main Subcategories of Science Found:

_____

_____

_____

_____

_____

_____

Second- and Third-Level Categories for Project Ideas:

_____

_____

_____

_____

_____

_____

Possible Project Topic:

_____

_____

_____

_____

Hint: This news article could be the basis for a great science fair project. In general, the main subcategories are biochemistry, medicine and health, and microbiology. One student developed a topic to determine how the amount of radiation used to irradiate meat affects the amount and types of bacteria that grow on meat. Also, the chemical composition of irradiated meat and its nutritional qualities versus nonirradiated meat could be studied. And what about mad cow disease? Does the irradiation process affect mad cow disease since it is said to be a protein-based disease? What other ideas can you develop from this story?

2. Challenge yourself to find three news articles on the Internet that concern some aspect about one topic of current interest or one new and expanding technology. Print them out. In the space provided, write down all the key words and science vocabulary terms. Don't forget to look up the definitions of science terms that you are not familiar with and write them next to the terms you selected from the article. Then try to summarize the article in about two sentences. Go back over your notes and create a list in the space provided of all applicable science fair project main subcategories as well as all second- and third-level categories. Finally, try to develop a project topic from one of your ideas.

Article #1

Science Vocabulary Terms Found and Defined:

_____

_____

_____

_____

Summary of Article:

_____

_____

_____

Main Subcategories of Science Found:

_____

_____

_____

_____

Second- and Third-Level Categories for Project Ideas:

_____

_____

_____

_____

Possible Project Topic:

_____

_____

_____

Article #2

Science Vocabulary Terms Found and Defined:

_____

_____

_____

_____

Summary of Article:

_____

_____

_____

Main Subcategories of Science Found:

_____

_____

_____

_____

Second- and Third-Level Categories for Project Ideas:

_____

_____

_____

_____

Possible Project Topic:

_____

_____

_____

Article #3

Science Vocabulary Terms Found and Defined:

_____

_____

_____

_____

Summary of Article:

_____

_____

_____

Main Subcategories of Science Found:

_____

_____

_____

_____

Second- and Third-Level Categories for Project Ideas:

_____

_____

_____

_____

Possible Project Topic:

_____

_____

_____

Local Topics of Interest

A great area to tap into is your own backyard. Certain topics and problems are ideal for your geographic location. For example, a vessel carrying home heating oil accidentally released thousands of gallons of oil into Massachusetts's Buzzards Bay in 2003. This event was a great environmental concern to those residents who live along the southeastern portion of Massachusetts and became a local topic of interest. A pair of students from Connecticut saw it as a unique opportunity to explore. After hearing about the unfortunate event, these students challenged themselves to read and learn as much about oil-spill cleanup solutions as possible. Through their research, they came across a key word and subject that caught their eye: _bioremediation_. They learned about bioremediation, a process where certain microbes are used to "eat" harmful gasoline, oil, fuels, and other inorganic contaminants to turn them into carbon and nitrogen by-products that are absorbed by plants. From this local topic of interest these students developed a project where they compared the effectiveness of various microbes in the process of bioremediation.

The following case study illustrates how one student found a science project on a subject close to her home.

PROJECT CASE STUDY #4: FINDING A PROJECT THROUGH LOCAL TOPICS OF INTEREST

Aquatic Killers: How Do Varied Nitrate, Phosphate, and Acidity Levels Affect the Growth and Development of Algae, Elodea, and Daphnia and How Do These Findings Compare to Ponds in South Plymouth, Massachusetts? by Colleen Muldoon

A Local Source of Inspiration for a Project Topic

When Colleen Muldoon was a small child, she used to swim all summer long in South Plymouth, Massachusetts, in a pond known for its clear, cool water and soft, sandy bottom. This pond was a favorite summer hangout for Colleen and her friends until a large algae bloom began to form several years later. Colleen was concerned about the future of the pond and decided to conduct research on the causes of algae blooms. Through her initial research, she learned that when over-abundant amounts of nitrogen and phosphorus in the forms of nitrate and phosphate are present in the water, eutrophication might occur, causing excessive growth of algae where living organisms in the pond are depleted of oxygen and sunlight and the pond essentially "dies." This initial research sparked more curiosity, and her science project began to take form.

An Environmental Project Topic "Blooms" into an Experiment

Colleen's research revealed that nitrates and phosphates are principal ingredients in soil fertilizer. She then theorized that the large algae bloom in her favorite pond might be due to the runoff of fertilizer in the groundwater from nearby homes. Therefore, she set up her experiment to examine the growth of daphnia and elodea in test tubes containing water with various amounts of fertilizer, namely, 0%, 0.1%, 0.2%, 0.5% and 1% concentrations to simulate the presence of nitrate- and phosphate-contaminated pond water. These benchmark samples would be compared to actual pond samples in the second phase of her experiment. To ensure consistent and accurate results, she used six test tubes for each concentration and living organism being studied, twelve in total.

Colleen monitored the color of the elodea leaves and level of activity of the daphnia daily and took measurements of the growth of the algae blooms in all of these test tubes with the use of a hemocytometer. Then she tested the pH levels in the test tubes each day. She measured all of her results daily for fifteen days and meticulously recorded her results. Then Colleen visited her favorite childhood pond along with four other area ponds and collected water samples to test for the actual amounts of nitrate and phosphate. Colleen compared these results with the results of her fertilizer benchmark sample group to estimate the possible condition of living organisms in the ponds.

Measurements and Analyses

Colleen's results from part one of her experiment indicated that when the concentrations of fertilizer increased, so did the amount of algae blooms. Consequently, at higher concentrations of nitrate and phosphate, the elodea plants decomposed and the daphnia population died off. She also determined which levels of nitrate and phosphate were "tolerable" to daphnia and elodea. Colleen learned that since nitrate can become nitric acid and phosphate can become phosphoric acid, when high concentrations of nitrate and phosphate were present in pond samples, the pH levels were also more acidic. Colleen found that the nitrate and phosphate levels in two of the ponds were exceedingly high, and she expected eutrophication to be the fate of these ponds. While her childhood pond could be in danger of eutrophication in the future, at present there still appeared to be plenty of life left in the pond. This conclusion could pave the way and provide

continued

continued

incentive to conduct further research to determine all the ways in which nitrate and phosphate levels occur in ponds so as to determine a means to prevent eutrophication.

Science Project Insight from Colleen

Colleen received finalist honors at the Massachusetts Science and Engineering Fair for her work. Colleen says that the best way to get started on a topic for the first time is to "ask yourself what puzzles you about the world around you. If you choose a topic that you can relate to and interests you, the science project experience is more enjoyable." Colleen feels that a student will be more tied to the outcome of a project and therefore do a more thorough job if he or she is genuinely interested in the topic. Further, she states that "it is essential to stay on top of your deadlines and experimental observations." Most important, she says, "When analyzing your experiment and drawing conclusions, be precise with your data results and try to relate as much of your findings as you can back to your research."

Of course, you don't have to wait for a major event in your community to find a local topic of interest. Look at the local resources in your area. Look at issues that affect the everyday life of the residents. Identify the main industry. All of these localized resources can provide a source of inspiration for a science project topic along with referrals to mentors who can help you with your topic. For example, you might find that your region contains a large mosquito population during a certain month. This issue alone might inspire you to explore alternative means for mosquito repellents that are not harmful to your community.

— EXERCISES —

1. Name an environmental issue that affects your state or region.

_____

_____

2. Name a natural resource that your state or region contains.

_____

_____

3. Name a major industry in your state or region.

_____

_____

4. Name a major manufacturing business in your state or region and its channel of trade.

_____

_____

In the corresponding space below, try to categorize your previous answers under one of the fourteen main project subcategories. Try to develop second- and third-level topics into workable science fair project topics.

1. Main Subcategories of Science Found:

_____

_____

_____

_____

Second- and Third-Level Categories for Project Ideas:

_____

_____

_____

_____

Possible Project Topic:

_____

_____

2. Main Subcategories of Science Found:

_____

_____

_____

_____

Second- and Third-Level Categories for Project Ideas:

_____

_____

_____

_____

Possible Project Topic:

_____

_____

3. Main Subcategories of Science Found:

_____

_____

_____

_____

Second- and Third-Level Categories for Project Ideas:

_____

_____

_____

_____

Possible Project Topic:

_____

_____

4. Main Subcategories of Science Found:

_____

_____

_____

_____

Second- and Third-Level Categories for Project Ideas:

_____

_____

_____

_____

Possible Project Topic:

_____

_____

Research a major science-related news story that involves something that happened in or concerned your state or region in the past two years. Scan the article to identify all key words and science vocabulary terms. (Look up the definitions of science terms that you are not familiar with and write them next to the terms you selected from the article.) Then try to summarize the news story in about two sentences. Go back over your notes and create a list in the space provided of all applicable science fair project main subcategories as well as all second- and third-level categories. Finally, try to develop a project topic.

Science Vocabulary Terms Found and Defined:

_____

_____

_____

_____

Summary of Article:

_____

_____

_____

Main Subcategories of Science Found:

_____

_____

_____

_____

Second- and Third-Level Categories for Project Ideas:

_____

_____

_____

_____

Possible Project Topic:

_____

_____

Visit a Science Fair or Attend a Science Fair Workshop

A great way to come up with a project idea is to surround yourself with science fair projects. If you are planning a project for the following year's science fair, you might want to check out the current year's school, town, state, or regional science fair nearest you. You will get to see how a science fair project is put together, what goes into it, and the level and quality of work done by middle and high school students in your area—the likes of which you will be competing with in the following year's science fair.

How do you know which projects are good examples to focus on for inspiration? It's easy. The judges have done all the work for you. Look for projects that the judges have selected as finalists. Analyze only those finalist projects in your age group and level of competition for the following year. What made these projects finalists? Did they focus on a new technology, problem, issue of current interest, or novel approach to an ongoing problem? How much work went into these projects? How did each finalist formulate his or her experiment? Did any of the finalists work with a mentor? How did they graph and present their data? How were the backboards for these projects designed? It's okay to take along a notebook so that you can jot down what inspired you or ideas that you found interesting. Further, if available for the public, be sure to pick up a few project abstracts so that you can review them and use them as a reference.

A WORD OF CAUTION

While it is beneficial to visit a science fair to see what goes into a winning science fair project and get ideas, do not attend for the purpose of copying another student's work. Not only would this be plagiarism but you would not achieve any success by showing up at the following year's science fair with an identical project. Science fair administrators and judges easily remember winning entries and will disqualify you if they sense you copied another student's work.

If you live in a remote area and cannot get to a science fair, or if you need a project for the current academic year, just log onto the Internet and conduct a search for your local, state, or regional science fair, or one in another state. There are plenty of Web sites that feature virtual science fairs. Many state and regional science fairs have their own Web sites, and some contain project abstracts of student contestants from the most recent science fair. While you may not be able to view the detailed steps of these projects, you should be able to get a sense of the level of work required.

Be aware that you are surrounded by science fair project ideas every day. Keep your eyes open and pay attention to the world around you. Use the exercises in this chapter. And remember that the best project idea for you is the one that you find most interesting.

3

MOVING ON TO THE NEXT STAGE: CONDUCTING MORE RESEARCH AND MAKING CONTACTS

THE GAME PLAN

To understand the rules and guidelines for science project subject matter for initial approval, and to learn how to make contacts with resources so that you have a good understanding of your topic and what you can achieve with it. Also, to know how to present your project proposal for final approval by your teacher, adviser, and Scientific Review Committee so that you can get started.

Know the Rules and Deadlines

Before you do anything else with your project topic, you should obtain a copy of the book of rules and guidelines for the science fair in which you plan to enter your project. Also, be sure to get a schedule of all pertinent deadlines for submitting your project application and any necessary forms required by the science fair. Your teacher or mentor should have a copy available for you to use. Read through the information carefully so that you will have a handle on the who, what, why, when, and how of getting your project approved and registered correctly with your science fair. At this point, you should get in the habit of taking notes on everything you will be learning and doing on your project.

Start a Project Journal

Before you begin working on your project, you should purchase a notebook with a pocket folder in which to record and organize most of what you are learning about your project. The notebook should contain information such as contacts you make, their place of business, the date you made contact with them, and any information, articles, or advice requested or received. With a **journal**, you will be able to manage your initial investigation more efficiently and will be in a better position to present your preliminary project proposal to your science teacher or adviser so that you can formulate a research plan for submission to the **Scientific Review Committee** (SRC) of your local science fair. Continue to use your journal throughout your report to record your hypothesis statement and experimental plan, to keep forms you are required to fill out for research approval, and to keep all recorded observations, photos, numerical data, diagrams, flowcharts, and other details that you will be gathering as you move along with your project.

Use your journal to record everything that happens in connection with your project, and be sure to date every entry so that you can easily refer back to various steps in your research more easily. Plan to record information about your project on a daily basis. Write about all the small things you do in connection with your project. Even if all you did for the day was surf the Internet or fill out permission forms, make sure you keep track of this information in your journal. You will be amazed to find that if you enter information on a daily basis, it will keep you motivated to work on your project and will keep you organized and on track. There is another benefit to keeping a great journal: it will help you write your report.

Sample Items to Include in Your Journal

1. Articles on your topic.

2. Sources of information.

3. Names of contacts, their official titles, places of business, addresses and phone numbers, dates of attempted contact, and copies of letters sent. If the contacts responded, the information you obtained from them and whether you received other referrals or possible mentors; advice they provided, books or resources they sent, and appointments to meet or chat with them in the future.

4. Notes about places you have visited, lectures or conferences you have attended, and interviews you have conducted.

5. Notes on supplies and equipment needed to perform your research and experimentation.

6. Contact information on where to obtain these materials and/or schools, colleges, or research facilities where you might be able to borrow supplies or equipment and/or conduct your research.

7. A checklist of all required forms you will need prior to beginning your research.

8. Skills you will be required to learn or develop and notes on the progress you have made in developing these skills.

9. How you developed your plan for experimentation and why you think this is the best plan to carry out your objective for your project.

10. Detailed notes on how your experiment was conducted including the variables that were tested and the controls that were used. Detailed information about different phases in your experiment including problems and surprise results.

11. All data results from your experiment whether or not they support your hypothesis and conclusions you have drawn from these results.

Having trouble organizing your project journal to include these items? See Appendix C in the back of this book for suggestions on how to organize sections in your project journal and forms that can help you keep track of different kinds of information. Feel free to duplicate these forms for use in your journal.

Project Limitations, Rules, Guidelines, and Forms

Once you have decided on a suitable topic, you will need to go through a few initial research steps as well as gain approval for your project. Most importantly, it is essential to look carefully at the topic you have selected to determine the amount of time you need to put in before the science fair deadline. It is also necessary to determine whether it is feasible to work with the project at all, given the strict rules that apply to subject matter, resources you will need, and possible expenses. Also, keep in mind that most science fairs are held annually from late February through late April, and most of them require that you complete an application form along with a science fair project proposal and research plan for review by their SRC no later than the preceding November or December.

Scientific Review Committee and Institutional Review Board Forms

The SRC is comprised of fair directors and scientific personnel who review information about your project, such as the subject matter you are studying and your research plan, including the materials you will use and where you will conduct your work, to determine if you are in compliance with rules established by your local Intel ISEF–affiliated science fair. It is usually mandatory that you submit this information, since most state and regional science fairs are feeder fairs to the Intel International Science and Engineering Fair. They are required to follow certain guidelines that govern the type of research you can do on your topic, how you do it, and where you do it. The purpose of the rules is to protect the safety of student researchers, human and animal subjects being studied (if applicable), as well as to comply with local and federal regulations governing research. You will need to look carefully at the amount of time you have to carry out your tentative project, and you will need to have your project proposal and plan for research and experimentation worked out well in advance of the late fall deadlines. Failure to do so may result in disqualification of your project.

So where do you start? You should plan to meet with your science teacher or adviser very early on in the process to discuss your proposed science fair project and research plan, in order to determine whether it is permissible under the rules and guidelines established by your science fair and whether you might need to modify your topic. Some subjects are considered part of a highly protected class in which strict rules apply. This class broadly includes the following subjects: vertebrate and nonvertebrate animals; human subjects; recombinant DNA; human and animal tissues; pathogenic agents, including bacteria, fungi, and mold; controlled substances and chemicals; mutagenic agents; carcinogenic agents; infectious agents; and hazardous materials or devices and controlled substances.

For projects involving these subjects, you are required to complete additional forms for project prescreening and approval by the SRC and possibly by an Institutional Review Board at your school or science fair. (If your project is going to involve the study and use of human subjects in a biomedical or behavioral way, additional forms need to be completed for review by the Institutional Review Board.) See Appendix D for sample forms used at most Intel ISEF–affiliated science fairs.

Human Subjects

Every Intel ISEF feeder fair has an **Institutional Review Board** (IRB) that is responsible for reviewing projects involving human subjects to evaluate the possibility for physical or psychological risk. You will need to fill out a Human Subjects Form (in all cases), an Informed Consent Form, and possibly a Qualified Scientist Form if there is more than a minimal risk to the human subjects you plan to study. Activities that have been defined as containing more than a minimal risk may seem somewhat harmless but are closely screened—for example, exercise, invasive questions for a behavioral study, and ingestion of any substances. Also, if any of your subjects are classified as part of a risk group, you will need to complete all the forms as well. Risk groups include children, pregnant women, people who have been diagnosed with a disease, the mentally handicapped, and the physically disabled.

The following case study covers a successful science project that was affected by the strict forms process.

PROJECT CASE STUDY #5: WORKING WITH HUMAN SUBJECTS— WORKING THROUGH STRICT GUIDELINES AND FORMS

Flex Your Memory: Will Cardiovascular Exercise Increase Short-term Auditory Memory Skills Better Than Relaxation (Meditative) Exercise? by Sheela Chandrashekar

"Meditating" on a Behavioral Science Project Topic

Sheela Chandrashekar became curious about the effects and benefits of meditation while observing her parents practice yoga to release tension after a stressful day. At home and in the library, Sheela saw many magazines and books pushing the benefits of proper breathing, meditation, and stretching for good health. With all of this information surrounding her, Sheela assumed that meditation was the best way for a person to maintain good health. However, on a daily basis, she also saw numerous television commercials, news articles, and reports touting vigorous cardiovascular exercise as being the best way to maintain good health.

Since rigorous exercise seemed so different from meditation, Sheela wondered if one was ultimately better than the other. While thinking about this subject, Sheela recalled that many of her colleagues at school who were always healthy and active seemed to have better attendance records and higher test scores, while other colleagues who were sedentary or were sometimes absent from school with a cold or some other common illness did not fare as well on test scores. After thinking about the positive effects that good health could have on mental activities, she decided to focus her project topic on determining whether cardiovascular exercise or meditation was better for increasing short-term memory. As an outgoing teenager who likes to work with people, Sheela took advantage of her curiosity and people skills to start a science fair project where she could interact with human subjects.

Working with Human Subjects

Since Sheela's project involved the use of human subjects, she was required to follow strict guidelines concerning experimentation. Sheela conducted her project under the guidance of her high school biology teacher and physical education teacher. Because her experiment involved exercise,

continued

continued

which is an activity that is characterized as being more than a minimal risk, Sheela had to complete numerous forms to gain project approval. Sheela's forms were submitted to the Massachusetts Science and Engineering Fair's Scientific Review Committee. After several phone calls between her science teacher and the fair's director, her research was approved. Her research plan called for the study of eighteen volunteer high school students between the ages of fourteen and eighteen, of the same aptitude (based on school records), who were free of breathing problems and health-related difficulties. These students were divided into three groups of six people per group. One group was tested on an auditory memory test after cardiovascular physical exercise, the second group was given the same test after meditative exercises, and the last group (the control group) was given the test without any prior physical or meditative exercise.

On the first day of the experiment, the control group was required to take an auditory memory test that Sheela labeled Test A, which consisted of twelve sets of numbers, ten sentences, and ten words. Increasing in length and difficulty, these numbers, sentences, and words were read aloud to the control group. Then the subjects were asked to write down the order of the numbers, sentences, and words from memory within a five-minute time frame. Finally, the subjects sat idly for five minutes and were then given a second auditory memory test, labeled Test B, which was similar to Test A. As in the first test, the students were asked to recall on paper the order of numbers, sentences, and words in five minutes. At the completion of the test, Sheela asked her control group of volunteers whether physical or meditative exercise was part of their daily routine. Their responses were recorded.

On the second day of the experiment, Sheela worked with the next group of volunteers. Like the control group, this group was required to take the auditory memory test that Sheela labeled Test A. Then these students were required to perform an initial two-minute warm-up walk around the perimeter of the gymnasium, followed by two minutes of jumping jacks, three minutes of running in place, and a three-minute cool-down walk around the perimeter of the gymnasium. Right after their cool-down walk, this group was given the second auditory memory test, labeled Test B. Once again, the students were asked to recall on paper the order of numbers, sentences and words in a five-minute period. At the completion of the test, Sheela asked this group of volunteers whether physical or meditative exercise was part of their daily routine. Their responses were recorded.

On the third day of the experiment, Sheela worked with the last group of volunteers. Like the other groups, this group was required to take the auditory memory test that Sheela had labeled Test A. These students were then required to perform a meditative exercise task. The subjects sat in their chairs with their eyes closed, feet flat on the floor, and hands resting on their thighs. They were asked to relax for about two minutes and imagine something peaceful and serene, such as ocean waves washing onto the shore. The group was then asked to take in a slow, steady, continuous breath of air through the nose to the count of five seconds. The subjects were asked to hold in the breath of air for twenty seconds, followed by slowly exhaling the air through the mouth over ten seconds. This breathing exercise was repeated five times. After the breathing exercises, this group was given the second auditory memory test, labeled Test B. Once again, the students were asked to recall on paper the order of numbers, sentences, and words within a five-minute period. At the completion of the test, Sheela asked them whether physical or meditative exercise was a part of their daily routine. Their responses were recorded.

Once Sheela collected all of her data, she arranged them into tables and performed several statistical analyses. After Sheela was able to remove and isolate those factors that may have skewed her data, she concluded that her results indicated that physical exercise increases short-term

continued

continued

auditory memory skills only slightly more than meditative exercise. However, both had a positive effect on short-term auditory memory and proved to be more effective than no activity at all (as was demonstrated by the control group). Sheela theorized that the results might have something to do with increased intake of oxygen by the test subjects through vigorous exercise and deep breathing with meditation.

Science Project Insight from Sheela

For students doing a project for the first time, Sheela strongly encourages them to plan ahead as soon as the new school year begins or even as early as summer so that all necessary research forms can be obtained and completed. Sheela also agrees that it is very important to pick a subject of interest to you. As she states, "I love working with children and I enjoy observing people, so I developed a project that combines these two factors." In conclusion, Sheela encourages other students to "be confident in yourself, believe in your project, and don't be afraid to have fun.... Science can be fun too!"

Nonhuman Vertebrate Animals

The Intel ISEF and all of its affiliated fairs establish strict guidelines concerning nonhuman vertebrate animals. Most science fair boards encourage students to explore all other possible alternatives for experimentation before resorting to the use of animals. Sometimes you can substitute plants, insects, cell and tissue cultures, or even mathematical or computer models. However, if there is no other substitute for experimentation, then you must follow all the rules and guidelines established, including the completion of all proper forms for experimentation with nonhuman vertebrate animals. Most Intel ISEF–affiliated science fairs require that you complete a Nonhuman Vertebrate Animal Form, an extremely detailed description of methods and procedures to be used through an Attached Research Plan, as well as a Qualified Scientist or Designated Supervisor Form. When performing animal research, you are also subject to all local, state, and federal regulations. So, it is extremely important to consult with your science teacher or adviser concerning all arrangements that will need to be made ahead of time and all necessary forms that must be filled out for your project's approval, such as those forms required by the institution where you will conduct the research and those forms required by law. The reason for all these rules and guidelines is to protect the welfare of animals and to provide them with humane treatment for their greatest comfort and well-being. See Appendix D for sample forms used at most Intel ISEF–affiliated science fairs.

Pathogenic Agents, Human and Nonhuman Vertebrate Animal Tissues, Recombinant DNA, Controlled Substances, and Hazardous Substances and Devices

Research involving disease-causing agents (pathogenic agents) or potential disease-causing agents must be performed under the guidance of a qualified scientist or designated supervisor in an institutional laboratory or school (in some cases, if there are adequate facilities available). With projects involving pathogenic agents, in addition to all the usual forms that need to be completed, you must fill out a Registered Research Institutional/Industrial Setting Form and supplement your research plan with specific information on the procurement of any pathogenic or potentially pathogenic agents. See Appendix D for sample forms used at most Intel ISEF–affiliated science fairs.

Research involving human and nonhuman vertebrate animal tissues may need to be performed under the guidance of a qualified scientist or designated supervisor, so check with your teacher or adviser ahead of time. In addition to all the usual forms, you may need to complete a Registered Research Institutional/Industrial Setting Form if you conduct your research in an institutional laboratory, and you will need to complete a Human and Nonhuman Vertebrate Animal Tissue Form to explain the procurement of the tissues you plan to study if they are coming from a research institution, biological supply house, or individual scientist. See Appendix D for sample forms used at most Intel ISEF–affiliated science fairs.

Note that research involving recombinant DNA, controlled substances, or hazardous substances and devices all require special arrangements, expert assistance, and completed forms prior to starting your research. If your project involves any of these types of materials, be sure to check with your teacher and adviser well before the deadlines for submitting your research plan so that you have everything in place.

Before you meet with your teacher or adviser to finalize and submit your project idea, research plan, and required forms (whether or not your project involves a protected class of subject matter), it is a good idea to do some initial reading on your topic and attempt to make some contacts pertaining to your subject. The purpose of this initial reading is to gather as much preliminary information as possible so that you will be able to talk informatively when you present your topic for approval by your teacher, adviser, SRC, or IRB at your local science fair.

You can begin by conducting a simple search of your topic on the Internet, as well as in scientific abstracts and periodicals. Spend about two hours a day for a week conducting this initial research. Read as many articles as you can. Try to identify at least one individual connected to the subject that you are reading about who would be able to advise you on specific resources, supplies, and equipment that you will need and who might serve as a mentor.

Identify and Make Contact with Key Resources

It is extremely beneficial to try to find at least one individual who you can talk to about your topic. A knowledgeable source can steer you in the right direction and will have good ideas about what can be done with your topic. How do you identify such a person when reading an article? It's easy. Find the name of the person who authored the article and make note of any references to scientists, engineers, technicians, professors, or doctors. Try to find a telephone number, e-mail address, or physical address for this person's place of business where you can contact him or her. (The author of the article may be able to assist you there.) Also, pay attention to names of universities, organizations, laboratories, and businesses mentioned in the article. If you cannot find the name of an individual, chances are good that you can contact the institutions named in the article and ask to speak with someone there who can help you.

Once you have found at least one resource, try to connect with this party by telephone, e-mail, fax, or regular mail. Remember to be polite and show respect and gratitude for the person's time and any information that he or she might provide. Be sure to explain that you are a student working on a science fair project under a deadline, and discuss the plans you have in mind for your project.

Ask your contacts for their advice and suggestions on what can be reasonably done with your idea. Ask them for literature that they might be able to recommend on your topic and for referrals with a connection to an institution or university. Perhaps one of your resources might even be able to let you know about other facilities or equipment that might be donated or made accessible to you in carrying out your research and experiment. Don't be shy! Remember that if you approach your contacts in a courteous and professional manner, you have nothing to lose and everything to gain. You may also find that your contacts will be glad to help, especially if your topic relates to their own specialty, products, technologies, or ideas. The important part of this step is that it will help you to save time and hone in on the specific information that you need.

You can use the format on the following page as a model for a letter or e-mail message that you can send to potential contacts.

American Nutraceutical Association
5120 Selkirk Drive
Suite 100
Birmingham, AL 35242

Dear Director:

I am a high school freshman working on a science fair project for my state's annual science and engineering fair in March, which is only six months away. I would be most grateful if you could provide me with your advice and/or suggestions concerning the following matter:

The topic I would like to work with concerns the effectiveness of the blue-green alga *Spirulina (Arthrospira)* in preventing infection by *E. coli*. Through my research, I came across an article in your publication, the *Journal of the American Nutraceutical Association*, Vol. 5, No. 2, Spring 2002, entitled "The Potential Application of Spirulina as a Nutritional and Therapeutic Supplement in Health Management," which mentioned research on the immunomodulation effects of *Spirulina* in the diet of chickens. The research indicated that the *E. Coli* bacteria were substantially cleared from the bloodstream of an infected chicken just thirty minutes after injection.

I would like to explore and expand upon these findings in my science fair project, and I was wondering if you would be able to either advise me in any way on how I might go about my research, or supply the name of a referral working in this field who might be able to advise me in developing my project objective or in creating my experimental plan. Additionally, any articles on the subject or any references to Web sites where I can obtain more information would be very helpful.

Since I need to provide my science teacher with my project proposal and research plan by November, please reply at your earliest convenience. Thank you very much for your time and help.

Sincerely,

Student Name

Finding a Mentor

While making contact with key resources, one of your objectives should be to find someone who will be willing to mentor you on your project. One of the best-kept secrets of students who have had a very successful science fair project experience is their affiliation with a mentor who is a professional scientist, engineer, or technician. A mentor can help in many ways, not only in the initial stages of your project but most importantly in assisting you in locating materials and equipment you will need, and possibly enabling you to carry out your experimentation at a university, private laboratory, or other testing facility. Students with a mentor often have a significant advantage over other students. This is especially true at the high school level. If your goal is to make it to the top science fair competition in your state or the Intel International Science and Engineering Fair, you really should consider making contact with a mentor.

Presenting Your Project Proposal to Your Teacher or Mentor

Somewhere between finding your topic, conducting initial research, making contacts, and preparing your actual research plan for final approval, you should plan to meet with your teacher or adviser. The purpose of this meeting is to discuss your project proposal and ideas for research and experimentation so that your teacher can determine whether your project idea is feasible. He or she will be able to help you hone in on the most important aspect of your project and determine if you will need to further modify your topic, objective, or research plan. He or she may even steer you in a different direction if your project topic appears to be too difficult or unrealistic. Your teacher will also be able to determine if you need to fill out special forms to carry out your research in the event you are working with subject matter that falls into a special protected class as we discussed earlier in this chapter.

Use this meeting wisely, ask questions, take notes, and make sure that you and your teacher have a meeting of the minds as to what you are planning to do with your project. You should be able to converse freely about the subject you want to study. Have notes or information ready from at least one contact or resource about your project topic. It would also help if you had a hypothesis statement prepared, a basic research plan worked out for your project, and some ideas on how to carry out your objective. (The following chapter will help you get to this point.)

Once your teacher or adviser has approved your project, it will be submitted to your local, state, or regional science fair for approval along with your project application form. If you have the option of selecting the main subcategory into which you would like to enter your project, be sure to choose the proper category with your teacher or mentor. It is usually easy to determine the category where your project belongs, but sometimes it may be difficult. For example, if you planned to do a project on human prosthetic limbs and joints, in which you study the physics of how artificial joints wear after a period of time, in which category would your project belong? Well, if your project emphasized the amount of friction in a joint, it would probably be a physical sciences project. But if you began to discuss the biodegradability of the device, your project might be more appropriately placed in the life sciences category. The wrong choice could hurt your outcome in the competition. In summary, be sure to discuss all these important issues with your teacher or mentor so that you can move forward with a research plan that is feasible and in compliance with rules and regulations.

4

STATING YOUR HYPOTHESIS, DEVELOPING YOUR RESEARCH PLAN FOR EXPERIMENTATION, AND CONDUCTING YOUR EXPERIMENT

THE GAME PLAN

To formulate a hypothesis and a procedure for testing your hypothesis through an experiment, and to plan how the experiment will be carried out through time frames, variables, and controls. Also, to plan the number of experimental trials that will be needed in order to arrive at a valid conclusion, and to determine how the results will be measured and recorded.

At this stage, you already have a project topic in mind and have conducted enough initial research to have arrived at a hypothesis. While getting to this stage, you should have found out what is already known about this topic, made some contacts with resources you found through your research, and collected some ideas about the direction of your project. This is a very important and exciting time in the course of your project, and you will need to put sufficient time and preparation into this stage, since it will significantly affect the rest of your project.

Start by taking a look at your topic, and plug it into the framework of the scientific method that we talked about in chapter 1. Here, you will notice that we are at stages 2 and 3: stating a hypothesis and formulating an objective to investigate your topic and test your hypothesis.

Stating Your Hypothesis in a Meaningful Way

A **hypothesis** is your prediction of the outcome of your experiment—your estimated solution to the problem or question you have proposed. Your hypothesis is an informed and logical statement about the expected outcome of your project based on what you know about the topic through preliminary research. In general, a good hypothesis statement starts with a well-stated purpose, problem, or inquiry as your project topic. For example, suppose you had an interest in agricultural science and researched the following general information about this topic:

Research: Certain crop diseases such as tan spot leaf fungus affect wheat when this crop is weakened due to certain environmental stresses, one of which may be prolonged periods of exposure to excess moisture. Tan spot leaf fungus may have a better chance at survival on wheat than barley and will recur with each growing season of wheat, assuming environmental conditions remain constant.

Suppose you conducted the above research and came up with the following topic: Can tan spot leaf fungus in wheat be eliminated? How would you answer this inquiry? Your topic may be too broad and poorly stated for what you want to investigate.

"I believe that tan spot leaf fungus can be eliminated" is not a good hypothesis statement. It gives no basis for the purpose of the project and provides no clear statement of what it is that you want to prove or disprove. Further, a project topic and a hypothesis this broad introduce other factors that may not have been part of what you were originally thinking about and may send you off course in the rest of your project. This can also open the door to inquiries and challenges by science fair judges that you may not be prepared for.

Compare and contrast the previously stated topic with the following project topic:

Topic: Can tan spot leaf fungus in wheat be eliminated through various crop rotations?

Based on existing research and in answering your project inquiry, a good way to state your hypothesis would be as follows:

Hypothesis: Since barley is not susceptible to tan spot leaf fungus, I believe that rotating and interchanging wheat and barley crops after each harvest will eliminate or reduce the risk of recurring tan spot leaf fungus in future harvests of wheat.

See the difference? Sometimes reviewing your initial research and restating a clearer and more precise project topic will result in a more effective hypothesis statement.

— EXERCISES —

Take a look at the following five project topics and formulate an effective hypothesis statement for each one. If you have trouble honing in on a hypothesis statement, try to restate the topic in a clearer and more precise manner so that a hypothesis can be developed. (If necessary, conduct some initial research on the Internet for the project topics.)

1. Which acne treatment—salicylic acid, benzoyl peroxide, or sulfur—works best in eliminating acne?

Hypothesis:

_____

_____

2. What are the effects of altitude on plant growth?

Hypothesis:

_____

_____

3. Does studying with Irlen overlays or Irlen filters affect memory ability?

Hypothesis:

_____

_____

4. Does the level of pH in the stomach affect the body's ability to digest and absorb certain vitamins?

Hypothesis:

_____

_____

5. What means of preservation keeps milk freshest?

Hypothesis:

_____

_____

Now take a look at your own proposed project topic and write down your hypothesis statement.

_____

_____

Look back through your initial research and determine if other hypothesis statements could be formed if your project topic were stated differently. See how many variations you can come up with so that you will have a few options to discuss with your teacher or adviser prior to submitting your project proposal.

Variations on My Project Topic:

_____

_____

_____

_____

_____

Alternative Hypothesis Statements:

_____

_____

_____

_____

_____

Developing a Meaningful Objective or Goal for Your Research and Experimentation

In general, your objective should be to address the most important aspect of your topic and define what you are searching for and trying to prove or disprove. Then you will need to choose a research plan that will reliably provide the answers. It should include an outline of the best experiment you can realistically carry out (given your resources) to achieve the results you are seeking.

There are three major questions that you will need to keep in mind while developing your plan for experimentation:

1. What do you want to investigate or prove?

2. What will you need to do in order to accomplish this?

3. Is this feasible, given your resources and time frames?

Let's look at our topic: *Can tan spot leaf fungus in wheat be eliminated through various crop rotation patterns?* There are several different ways that this topic can be developed through a research plan. Let's see if we can find the most important aspect about this topic so that we can isolate what we should be seeking. Here are some possibilities:

1. Determining whether crop rotation has any positive effect in eliminating tan spot leaf fungus

2. Determining the efficiency of wheat crop rotation based on wheat crop quality

3. Determining if tan spot leaf fungus is eliminated in wheat through moving the crop around and planting barley in its place

4. Determining the crop rotation patterns needed to effectively eliminate tan spot leaf fungus

After you have listed various approaches to your project, choose one that you think will produce a reasonable and practical experiment. While all of the above objectives are good, you will need to work with one that can be turned into a practical experiment that can be carried out thoroughly and effectively so that meaningful measurements can be taken and sound conclusions can be made from these measurements.

Looking at these choices, it is easy to see that unless you have access to a farm where wheat and barley are grown, you will probably not be able to conduct your experiment on a large scale outdoors. The project will need to be scaled down proportionately and conducted perhaps in a greenhouse environment with a set number of plantings, some of which will already need to contain the tan spot leaf fungus. Therefore, you will need to determine if you can access a greenhouse to conduct your experiment, whether you will be able to obtain plantings containing the fungus, whether certain state or federal laws will allow you to work with the fungus, and whether you will have enough time to grow and observe all the plantings so that you will be able to collect data and draw meaningful conclusions.

To take another project example, if you wanted to *determine the efficiency of bioremediation to neutralize and clean up oil from a spill in a sea harbor,* you would need to organize an experiment that would allow you to measure the efficiency of various microorganisms in neutralizing the presence of oil in seawater. It would be difficult (not to mention illegal) to add oil to a body of water for the purpose of testing bioremediation over a short period of time, so a more practical thing to do would be to collect several large buckets of natural seawater that you could add home heating oil to along with your microorganism variable for testing in an environmentally safe area. Your objective would then be to study the effects of various microorganisms in the bioremediation of home heating oil. After you have organized your experiment, you must develop an experimental plan.

Developing an Experimental Plan

An **experimental plan** is a uniform, systematic approach to testing your hypothesis. When you begin this phase, you should make a step-by-step list of what you will do to test your hypothesis. To start, *correlate* (i.e., bring one thing into a reciprocal relationship with another) what you want to prove. Begin by selecting one thing to change in each **experiment**. Things that are changed are called **variables**. Correlation comes in with two or more variables: dependent and independent. The dependent variable is the one that is being measured; the independent variable is the one that is controlled or manipulated by the experiment.

For example, you may want to see whether the health and growth of a tomato plant (the dependent variable) is influenced by the amount of light the plant is exposed to (the independent variable). This correlation would be between the health of a plant and light exposure. Several other independent variables could be used instead, such as water, oxygen, carbon dioxide, and nitrogen levels. (Keep in mind that it is always important to limit the number of variables in an experiment so that the experimental results and the variables can be directly correlated.) However, for the sake of clarity, we will use only light as an independent variable. You should state how you will change your independent variable and how you will measure the amount of change. For example, you will need to determine the specific amount of light and water the tomato plants will be exposed to, how you will measure plant growth, and what you will compare your results to in order to draw a conclusion about whether the amount of light has any effect on plant growth. Once you have an idea worked out you need to organize it scientifically by identifying the experiment group and control group, the manner in which the experiment will be carried out, how data will be collected and the number of trials that will be repeated of the same experiment to ensure consistent and reliable results.

Establish a Control Group

An experimental group and a control group must be established. The control group provides you with a basis against which to compare the experimental group. For example, you may have an experimental group of tomato plants in a sunny window for two weeks that are watered periodically. At the end of the period, the plants have grown three inches and are very green. At this point, you may conclude that sunlight does indeed increase plant growth. But before you draw this conclusion, you should determine whether the tomato plants would have grown and become green without sunlight. Therefore, a control group of plants is needed.

The control group would be plants that are given the same treatment as the experimental ones, with the exception that they are not exposed to sunlight. If the outcome of the experiment were that there was a significant difference between the two groups, then you probably would be justified in concluding that tomato plant growth is influenced by the amount of sunlight the plant receives.

The experimental plan in this example is very simple, but it gives you an idea of the process of an experimental plan. In essence, the experimental plan advances from one stage to another in an organized fashion. Remember, however, that most experiments are not as simple as the one described here. Often, obstacles arise and other interesting characteristics of the subject are revealed. You may even discover existing differences in several trials with only one variable. In fact, this is a frequent occurrence, and it is an important reason why you must keep accurate data records (see chapter 5).

All of these factors need to be looked at in great detail before you can settle on a research and experimental plan to present to your teacher or adviser. Before you rush off with a topic and an idea for experimentation, do some preliminary research to determine how you can carry out your objective. Be sure to consult with your contacts and mentor often so that you will be able to come up with a specific objective that can be worked into a research and experimental plan. This way you will be thoroughly prepared when you meet with your teacher or adviser for final approval before sending off your plan to your science fair's Scientific Review Committee.

— EXERCISE —

Take a look at your project topic, hypothesis statement, and objective, and write down your experimental plan. Note your variables and control, how you plan to measure your results and the number of experimental trials that will be needed to obtain a reliable conclusion.

_____

_____

_____

_____

_____

Conducting Your Experiment

As soon as you receive official approval for your project research plan, you can start your experiment. The first step is to collect the materials you will need for the experiment and/or obtain permission to work in a laboratory or other professional environment. As you put your experimental plan into action, remember to collect accurate data results from repeated trials with the same variables and record all of your data for later analysis (see chapter 5 for this important next step). This will increase the accuracy of your results and conclusions. How many times do you need to repeat your experimental procedural plan? This depends on many different factors, not the least of which is your subject matter. However, regardless of the number of times you repeat your experiment, keep in mind that you need to maintain consistency among your variables throughout repeated trials when collecting your data.

Note: Appendix B lists science project supply companies that may be able to provide you with the supplies and equipment you need to carry out your experiment. However, if you have a mentor who is a professional scientist or engineer, you may already have the supplies and equipment you need through the mentor's affiliation with a university or company research laboratory.

How to Avoid a Failed Experiment

There are several reasons why an experiment may fail to validate a hypothesis, prove a point, or simply do what it was intended to do. Such reasons include mistakes in the way the experiment was carried out (procedural errors), a poor or incomplete final analysis, and an **erroneous hypothesis**.

Procedural Errors

To avoid procedural problems, you must be consistent and meticulous with your subject variables and controls and hold all of them steady for repeated trials. For example, in the experiment involving sunlight and tomato plants, if you gave the experimental group of tomato plants more water than the control group or planted them in a soil that contained more nitrogen, you would get artificial results. You would have failed to control or hold your variable constant. How can you determine whether it was the sunlight alone or in combination with other factors that made the experimental tomatoes flourish? The same problem with inconsistent maintenance of controls might apply if you were studying the behavior of your friends at a party for a psychological experiment. What would happen if you made your study obvious by taking notes or pictures? Your friends probably would be influenced by your behavior and would not act in their usual manner. In this case, as the saying goes, "you cannot measure an experiment without affecting the result." These examples involve manipulated experiments that would yield useless data. Of course, there are other procedural problems that can arise during an experiment, especially if poorly calibrated measuring instruments are used.

Poor Final Analysis

Even after a carefully controlled experiment is completed, errors can still occur. Such errors could result from an incorrect analysis of results. For example, if you concluded that a certain salve cures acne on the basis of tests that were conducted on female adolescents but not males, your final analysis would be inconclusive. While the salve may have worked on the females you tested, it may not work on females in different age groups or on males of all age groups. Other problems with final analysis may arise from mathematical errors or from data that are irrelevant to the topic.

Erroneous Hypothesis

When an experiment is completed, the results are sometimes quite different from those that were predicted. If this occurs, do not manipulate the results to fit the initial hypothesis. Often, it may be that the hypothesis was incorrect or vague to begin with and that the experimental results were accurate. If such problems occur in your project, you can salvage your work by finding out why the results were different than expected, or by explaining a new or unexpected observation or solution. This will show the judges that you have a good grip and understanding on the primary aspects that concern your project topic, including the control and handling of variables in experimentation, repeated trials, and the approach to reaching conclusions. This actually happens to be a judging criterion that many students overlook. If your experimental results are different from what you expected after several trials, take advantage of this situation by thoroughly analyzing and knowing why you received the results you did. (For more information about the criteria that judges look for, see chapter 7.)

Keep in mind that many scientific investigations do not support their specific goals. However, this does not weaken the value of these investigations. In fact, many experiments require repeated testing and exploration to understand a particular phenomenon. Sometimes unexpected experimental results lead to surprising discoveries and more interesting science projects!

5

MEASURING, RECORDING, ORGANIZING, AND PRESENTING DATA

THE GAME PLAN
To learn what to measure and how to analyze results and observations to form a valid conclusion.

Believe it or not, the most important aspect of your science fair project will be calculating, analyzing, and presenting your numerical data to provide a clear means for others to interpret your results and conclusions. Almost all science fair judges agree on this. Not only will you need to present your results with precision but you will need to be able to explain your results. So, let's get started on our journey into the world of science project data.

Basically, there are two types of data analysis: qualitative analysis and quantitative analysis. **Qualitative analysis** is a means of analysis that contains your overall observation; for example, what components were found in a sample, or whether an experimental group of plants performed better than a control group of plants. **Quantitative analysis** is based purely on measurements and always involves numbers—for example, how much of a given component is present in a sample, or how much the experimental group of plants grew in comparison to the control group.

Variables and controls can be measured quantifiably through any means of measurement such as a balance or scale, thermometer, ruler, computer, timer, speedometer, gauss meter, test kit, pH indicator, sound meter, number of correct answers on a questionnaire, preferences, behavior, and so on. While qualitative analysis is important for explaining your results, it is quantitative analysis that truly expresses your ability as a student scientist to interpret your data in a precise and objective way that will provide a useful means for others to understand your conclusions.

What You Need to Measure

You will need to know what needs to be measured while carrying out your experiment. In the last chapter we used a very basic example defining the dependent variable, independent variable, and control when we looked at whether the health and growth of a tomato plant (dependent variable) is influenced by the amount of light exposure (independent variable). In this example, a basic experiment could be developed where your experimental group of tomato plants is placed in a sunny window for two weeks and watered periodically while your control group of tomato plants is watered periodically but is not exposed to light. Your qualitative analysis might be that the plants exposed to sunlight performed better than the plants not exposed to sunlight. But your quantitative analysis, since it is based on numbers, provides a more precise analysis and comparison based on the amount of growth the experimental tomato plants experienced compared to the control group. You would base your quantitative analysis on the length and height of the experimental tomato plants and control plants, as measured with a ruler or other means, and on the number of new leaves or yellowed leaves on each plant, as measured through counting the number of leaves. All of these numerical measurements are recorded and are referred to as data.

How much data do you need for analysis and formulation of a valid conclusion? The answer varies, of course, based on what you are measuring and how feasible and practical it is to gather your data. But generally you will want to repeat several trials of the same experiment, using the same variables and controls from the same population distribution or group sample to maintain reliable and consistent results. Once all of your data are gathered, you can compile and organize them through the use of tables, graphs, and statistical analysis. Then you can use your organized data to make observations and conclusions about your project.

Tabulating and Graphing Basics

Data must be arranged so that a project observer or judge can quickly comprehend the results of a project at a glance. Tables are relatively simple to make and convey information with precision. Additionally, they form the basis for most graphs. The main points to consider are organization and coordination. For example, suppose you conducted a science project experiment where you were trying to determine which type of insulation, fiberglass or cellulose, maintained the most constant and even temperature during a weekend in December or January. For the sake of consistent and reliable results, you may have taken the temperature measurements of the attics of several homes with fiberglass and cellulose insulation every two hours during a twelve-hour period over two days. After you gathered all of your data, you might have averaged the temperatures of each insulation-type home tested at each specific measurement point during the day. The average hourly temperature of the fiberglass-insulated attics and the hourly temperature of the cellulose-insulated attics during a weekend in the month of December or January can be represented in tables like the following:

Fiberglass-Insulated Home Temperatures

Time	Average Attic Temperature (°F)
8:00 A.M.	46
10:00 A.M.	51
Noon	55
2:00 P.M.	57
4:00 P.M.	53
6:00 P.M.	51
8:00 P.M.	49

Cellulose-Insulated Home Temperatures

Time	Average Attic Temperature (°F)
8:00 A.M.	53
10:00 A.M.	54
Noon	56
2:00 P.M.	59
4:00 P.M.	57
6:00 P.M.	55
8:00 P.M.	52

If you want to see how either the fiberglass- or cellulose-insulated attic temperatures fluctuated during the day, you can do this by analyzing the table. But if you wanted to see at a glance how the temperatures changed, a graphic representation would be more effective.

A line graph may be used for this analysis. A **line graph** is comprised of two axes: the x, or horizontal, and the y, or vertical. The x-axis contains all the points for one set of data, and the y-axis contains all the points for the other set of data.

For example, in the first graph, you could label a range of fiberglass-insulated attic temperatures on the y-axis and label the times on the x-axis. After your axes are labeled, simply plot the points. Plotting involves matching each temperature with the corresponding time and marking them on the graph. For example, in the fiberglass-insulated homes, at 6:00 A.M., the average attic temperature was 45 degrees Fahrenheit, so you should locate and mark the point on the graph at which 6:00 A.M. and 45 degrees correspond. Then you would do this for the rest of the data and connect the points to complete the graph. This procedure would be repeated for the cellulose-insulated homes.

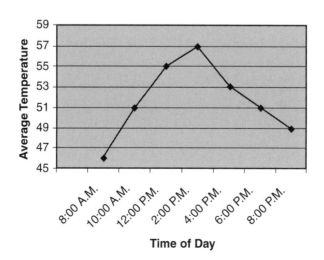

Fiberglass-Insulated Home Temperatures

Cellulose-Insulated Home Temperatures

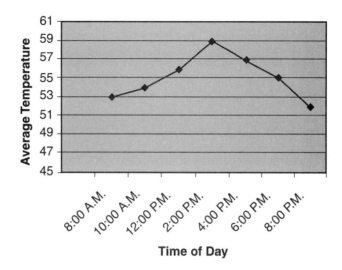

From these graphs, you can quickly see that the fiberglass-insulated attic temperatures rose modestly, peaked in the middle of the day, and fell during the evening, while the cellulose-insulated attic temperatures were slightly higher and more steady throughout the course of the day.

Another means for representing your data is through a bar graph. Suppose that you want to demonstrate the pH levels of water samples taken from various ponds. Again, you will use a horizontal and vertical axis to frame the table. The pond names can be listed along the horizontal axis and the pH levels along the vertical axis. Once you are finished labeling the axes, draw a bar going from the zero line for each pond sample up to the area on the y-axis that corresponds with its pH level as shown in the following diagram:

pH Levels of Area Ponds

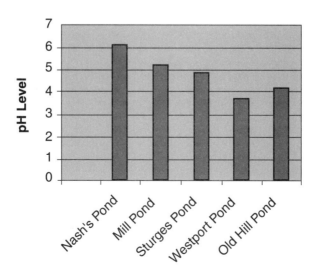

There are many other ways to graph your data besides the basic tables and bar and line graph methods already shown. Remember that graphing summarizes your results in a visual form that emphasizes the differences between data groups. The basic table and line graph method can help you determine whether there are notable differences in your measurements. This leads to a discussion of statistics, which is the preferred method that scientists use to analyze their data.

The Statistical Method

It is impossible to provide a thorough synopsis of statistics in this workbook. Math departments at colleges and universities teach numerous classes on this subject including probability, applied statistics, stochastic processes, biometrics, decision theory, linear models, variance, game theory, methods of sampling, and so on. Many students, especially those planning to compete in the Intel ISEF and other prestigious competitions such as the Intel Science Talent Search or the Siemens Westinghouse competition, often incorporate some of these advanced levels of statistics into their science fair projects. Some even build math and computer science fair projects around these statistical principles.

If you are in high school, you are strongly encouraged to read more on the subject of statistics, since your ability to accurately and effectively use statistical analysis in interpreting your quantitative data results will greatly enhance the success of your science fair project. If you are in middle school, you may not need these advanced methods yet, but you should know some basics. Therefore, the remainder of this chapter will discuss some very simple **statistical methods** to help you get a feel for how to calculate, present, and analyze your data results. Some of these applications include the mean, the median, the mode, frequency distribution, percentile, and standard deviation.

The **mean** is a mathematical average of your data. (You probably learned this method years ago when you were trying to figure out what your grade would be on your report card.) Statistically speaking, the mean is expressed as $\bar{x}$, where x is any rational number. The sum of your data numbers is denoted by the symbol Σ, which means "the summation of." This sum is then divided by the quantity of your data recordings, which is the symbol n. Thus, the mean is expressed as this formula:

$$\bar{x} = \frac{\Sigma x}{n}$$

For example, what if you wanted to find the mean fluoride level, in parts per million (ppm), from eleven different water departments?

Town Name	Fluoride Level (ppm)
A-Town	1.00
B-Town	1.75
C-Town	2.05
D-Town	0.75
E-Town	1.00
F-Town	1.01
G-Town	1.00

H-Town	1.55
I-Town	2.00
J-Town	1.00
K-Town	1.00
	$\sum(x) = 14.11$

Using the formula, you can express your results as follows: If $\sum(x) = 14.11$ and $n = 11$, then $\bar{x} = 14.11/11 = 1.28$. The figure 1.28 is the mean, or the mathematical average, of the eleven water departments.

GRAPHING SOFTWARE

Out of one hundred high school science fair projects recently analyzed at a prestigious state science fair competition on the East Coast, almost 75 percent of these projects not only incorporated the use of intermediate- to advanced-level statistics, but many employed the use of graphing software such as Microsoft Excel, CricketGraph, Harvard Graphics, and Kaleidograph. (Kaleidograph in particular appears to be a popular and preferred graphing program that you should consider learning if you plan to make it to the top level of science fair competition.) Graphing software can be useful when showing various relationships. For example, suppose you made a series of measurements of voltage distribution through a computer, as Lohith Kini did with his project for the Massachusetts State Science and Engineering Fair. Your recorded data could be input into a graphing software program whereby you could show your results through a sharp and attractive three-dimensional graph (see the figure). Graphing software can create awesome and professional-looking graphs that provide a great means for supporting your conclusions. Some of these programs are expensive, so it would be wise to see if your school or even a local college or university might have the software and allow you to use it.

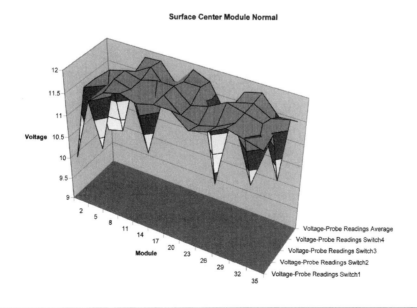

Surface Center Module Normal

While the mean provides us with the average of a set of data, sometimes it may not be the most useful statistic in assessing the measurement that best sums up and describes your data. This is usually the case when the lowest or highest measurements differ substantially from all the other measurements obtained. Sometimes scientists throw out the lowest and highest figures in an effort to obtain a truer mean from the data results. Other times they keep all of their measurements and use either the mode or the median to offer the best description of their data results.

The **mode** is the numerical value that occurs most frequently in your data results. In the example above, the numerical value that occurs most frequently is 1.00, which is a bit lower than the mean of 1.28. The **median** is the middle numerical value of your data results. The median is found by listing all of your data in ascending order from the lowest number to the highest. In this case, your numbers would be organized as 0.75, 1.00, 1.00, 1.00, 1.00, 1.00, 1.01, 1.55, 1.75, 2.00, 2.05. The middle value of this set of eleven numbers is 1.00; therefore, 1.00 is the median. If you are looking for the median in an even group of numbers, simply locate the middle two values and average them.

Now suppose that you collected samples from fifty water departments. While you might be able to generalize about the results with the mean, mode, and median, a better method might be needed for describing your data. One way of describing the results statistically is with a **frequency distribution**. This method is a summary of a set of observations showing the number of items in several categories. For example, suppose that the following fluoride levels were observed to be present in fifty samples:

Fluoride Level (ppm)	Frequency (f)
2.00	3
1.70	6
1.50	7
1.00	8
0.90	10
0.80	7
0.50	6
0.04	3
	$\Sigma f = 50n$

These results can then be graphed using a **histogram**, which represents your frequency distribution. Like a bar graph, your item classes are placed along the horizontal axis and your frequencies along the vertical axis. Then rectangles are drawn with the item classes as the bases and the frequencies as the sides. This type of diagram is useful because it clearly shows that the fluoride levels are normally at the 0.90 to 1.00 ppm mark (see diagram).

A **percentile** is the position of one value from a set of data that expresses the percentage of the other data that lie below this value. To calculate the position of a particular percentile, first put the values in ascending order. Then divide the percentile you want to find by 100 and multiply by the number of values in the data set. If the answer is not an integer (a positive or negative whole number), round up

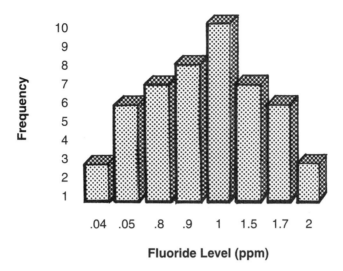

to the next position of the data value you're looking for. If the answer is an integer, average the data values of that position and the next higher one for the data value you're looking for.

For example, suppose that you want to test the fuel efficiency of eleven automobiles by measuring how many miles each car gets to a gallon of gasoline. You have recorded the following data for the average miles per gallon of each car: 17.6, 16.4, 18.6, 16.1, 16.3, 15.9, 18.9, 19.7, 19.1, 20.2, and 19.5. First, arrange the numbers in ascending order: 15.9, 16.1, 16.3, 16.4, 17.6, 18.6, 18.9, 19.1, 19.5, 19.7, and 20.2. Now suppose that you want to determine which car ranks in the ninetieth percentile. To calculate the ninetieth percentile for this data set, write this equation: $(90/100)(11) =$ 9.9. Since 9.9 is not an integer, round up to 10, and the tenth value is your answer. The tenth value is 19.7; therefore, the car that travels 19.7 miles per gallon of gasoline is in the ninetieth percentile, and 90% of the cars in your study are less gas efficient.

The **standard deviation** is a bit more complicated but is especially useful. The standard deviation works with the distribution of a group of data and measures the variations or spread that exists within the data. It explains the differences between the mean and each data value. The best way to explain the standard deviation is to look at the following density curve, which provides a mathematical model for the normal distribution of a group of data. This curve happens to be a bell-shaped symmetric curve, and the standard deviation can be explained on this curve through the **68–95–99.7 rule**, also known as the **empirical rule**.

This bell-shaped curve assumes that there is an even or normal distribution of data from the center of the curve (the mean), with 68 percent of the data lying one standard deviation away from the mean in both directions (darkest shaded area), 95 percent of the data lying two standard deviations away from the mean in both directions (the darkest shaded area plus the second darkest shaded area), and 99.7 percent of the data lying three standard deviations away from the mean in all directions (all shaded areas), accounting for the remainder of the data. Not all sets of data will create a perfect bell-shaped curve; sometimes the curves are very steep, lean to one

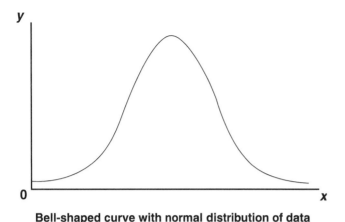

Bell-shaped curve with normal distribution of data

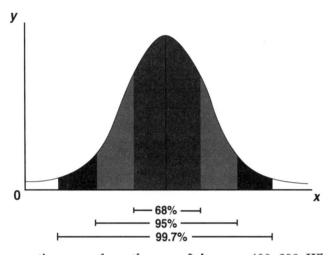

├── 68% ──┤
├── 95% ──────┤
├── 99.7% ──────────┤

side, or are very flat. The standard deviation simply tells how close all the data are to the mean. When most of your data are very close to the mean, the standard deviation is small and the result will be a very steep curve. (Note: If all the data results were the same, then the standard deviation would be zero.) When most of your data are very different from the mean, the standard deviation is large and the result will be a flatter or lower-shaped curve. Thus, the 68–95–99.7 rule, or empirical rule, applies only when you have a normal distribution of data.

For example, using the 68–95–99.7 rule, if the mean SAT math score for students at your local high school is 500 and the standard deviation is known to be 100, then what range should students be within when they are at 68 percent or one standard deviation away from the mean? Answer: 400–600. What range should they be within at 95 percent or two standard deviations away from the mean? Answer: 300–700. What range should they be within at 99.7 percent or three standard deviations away from the mean? Answer: 200–800.

Now that you have a handle on what a normal distribution looks like, you might be wondering how the standard deviation is calculated in the first place. It is calculated using the following formula:

$$\text{Standard Deviation} = \sqrt{\frac{\sum_{i=1}^{n}(x_i - \bar{x})^2}{n}}$$

Yes, the formula looks very scary, but when you break it down methodically, it is easy to understand. Let's look at the following example using our data we gathered from testing various automobiles to see how many miles each gets to the gallon. We collected the following data for our eleven vehicles: 15.9, 16.1, 16.3, 16.4, 17.6, 18.6, 18.9, 19.1, 19.5, 19.7, and 20.2. The first step in using our standard deviation formula is to calculate the average of our data:

$$\frac{15.9, 16.1, 16.3, 16.4, 17.6, 18.6, 18.9, 19.1, 19.5, 19.7, \text{and } 20.2}{11} = 18.03$$

Then we subtract each data result from the average data figure above and square the result:

$$18.03 - 15.9 = 2.13^2 = 4.55$$
$$18.03 - 16.1 = 1.93^2 = 3.72$$
$$18.03 - 16.3 = 1.73^2 = 2.99$$
$$18.03 - 16.4 = 1.63^2 = 2.66$$
$$18.03 - 17.6 = 0.43^2 = .185$$
$$18.03 - 18.6 = -.57^2 = .325$$
$$18.03 - 18.9 = -.87^2 = .757$$
$$18.03 - 19.1 = -1.07^2 = 1.14$$
$$18.03 - 19.5 = -1.47^2 = 2.16$$
$$18.03 - 19.7 = -1.67^2 = 2.79$$
$$18.03 - 20.2 = -2.17^2 = 4.71$$

Next we add the resulting numbers together and divide by the number of data results being studied:

$$\frac{4.55 + 3.72 + 2.99 + 2.66 + .185 + .325 + .757 + 1.14 + 2.16 + 2.79 + 4.71}{11} = 2.36$$

And then we take the square root of this number to achieve our standard deviation. Therefore,

$$\sqrt{2.36} = 1.54$$

and our standard deviation is 1.54, which is relatively low.

Other Means for Representing Data

Since every project is different, you may find that you will need other means for showing and explaining your data results. For example, if you need to refer to various stages of a science project experiment that was conducted over a long period of time where measurements may have been taken at various stages, a **time line** might be a better means of representing your data. Additionally, if you need to describe the results of a repeated process or a sequence and it is cumbersome to do so through text, a series of **flowcharts** may be useful and may make your project data results visually interesting. (See diagrams on the following page.)

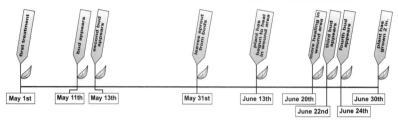

GROWTH RATE OF AGROBACTERIUM TUMEFACIENS INFECTED PLANT TREATED WITH A BETA-CAROTENE/WATER SOLUTION OVER A 2-MONTH PERIOD OF TIME

first treatment

bud appears

spreads bud buds

leaves sprout from buds

plant has begun to heal in wound area

more healing in wound area

third bud appears

fourth bud appears

plant has grown 2 in.

| May 1st | May 11th | May 13th | | May 31st | June 13th | June 20th | | June 30th |

June 22nd | June 24th

Time Line

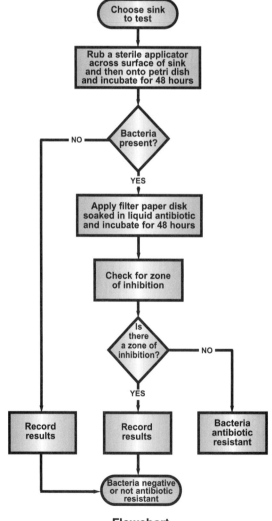

Do Household Sinks Harbor Antibiotic-Resistant Bacteria?

Choose sink to test

Rub a sterile applicator across surface of sink and then onto petri dish and incubate for 48 hours

Bacteria present?

NO

YES

Apply filter paper disk soaked in liquid antibiotic and incubate for 48 hours

Check for zone of inhibition

Is there a zone of inhibition?

NO

YES

Record results

Record results

Bacteria antibiotic resistant

Bacteria negative or not antibiotic resistant

Flowchart

Another means of graphical representation that makes data easily understood is the **pie chart**. Suppose that you are testing a specimen of blood to determine the percentage of its composition of erythrocytes, leukocytes, and thrombocytes. After several tests and microscopical observation, you conclude that the blood contains the following:

Cell Type	Composition
Erythrocytes	50.0%
Thrombocytes	38.0%
Leukocytes	12.0%
	$\Sigma = 100.00\%$

Note: Σ is a Greek symbol that means "the summation of."

The data can be represented in a pie chart:

Blood Composition

Each section represents a percentage of the pie. The pie chart format makes it easy to see that the leukocyte blood count is low in terms of its percentage of the total composition.

You will have to decide which technique works best for your type of data. You can usually express your results in tables, line and bar graphs, or a statistical method. However, there are occasions when only one technique will work. If you are dealing with numerous figures or classes of figures, a statistical method usually works best. For example, if you wanted to demonstrate the variation of test scores between boys and girls in the eighth grade, you would probably make your point clearer by using a statistical method, which would allow you to find the percentiles in which each student scored, the mean test score, and the standard deviation. Whatever technique you choose to use, make sure that it presents your numerical data clearly so that others can interpret your results and conclusions.

6

PREPARING YOUR DISPLAY: REPORT, ABSTRACT, AND BACKBOARD BASICS

THE GAME PLAN
To prepare a scientific research paper, abstract, and backboard for your display.

At this stage, you probably have a lot of research notes, data, graphs, photos, and drawings that you have been collecting since you began your project. The good news is that your science fair project is essentially complete. All that is left is explaining and summarizing your work so that others may be able to understand the purpose of your project, why it was researched, how the experiment was conducted, and your results and conclusions. All the parts are before you and it's time to put them together.

Due to guidelines established by the Intel ISEF, almost all state and regional science fairs have encouraged the use of the backboard as the display focal point. The backboard is accompanied by the other main display items, which are the report and the abstract, and can include other items that help to explain the project if they are permitted by your local, state, or regional science fair. However, the first thing that you should prepare is your report. Once the report is completed, the rest of the display is easy to put together.

The Report

The report is an extremely important part of the project. It should contain several main points about your project, such as the historical background of your subject, an introduction that states your purpose, a procedure that explains your research and means of acquiring information, your plan for organizing an experiment, and all the recorded data, diagrams, flowcharts, photos, conclusions, and other details that fully explain your project. While it may seem like a lot of work to prepare, it is not. Remember that journal you started months ago that contains summaries of the articles you read about your topic, daily notes you took about the progress you made, professionals you consulted, ideas you wrote about in planning and carrying out your experiment, materials you needed, and the data results you obtained from your experiment? Well, you will be pleased to know that all your meticulous notes are actually the ingredients for your report.

Organizing the Report

While the report is similar to a scientific research paper or a formal scientific abstract, it does not have to be lengthy in order to be good, but it does need to cover several main points about your project. Keep in mind that your report is your spokesperson when you are not with your project (for example, during preliminary judging at your science fair), so you will want it to be able to stand on its own apart from whatever oral presentation you plan to give on your project topic. Need a starting point? Just use the following outline as the basis for your report, then write a detailed summary under each section of the outline:

1. Title Page

2. Contents

3. Abstract (A project summary that is about 250–300 words long. See text that follows for more information.)

4. Purpose

5. Hypothesis Statement

6. Introduction (Historical Background of Subject Matter—i.e., a general statement of what is already known about this subject, why you chose your topic, and what you planned to accomplish with this topic.)

7. General Research Conducted (may include a summary of articles read, professionals consulted, etc.)

8. Objective for Project

9. General Procedure for Experiment(s) (a detailed description of what was being tested, the variables and controls used, materials and supplies utilized, how the experiment was carried out, and how data were recorded)

10. Data Results (graphs, tables, charts, diagrams, photos, drawings)

11. Conclusion

12. Sources (a list of mentors or professionals who you consulted or who assisted you in your research and experiment)

13. Footnotes

14. Bibliography

15. Appendixes (may include any additional information gathered that will help to explain your project and the work you conducted, such as articles, letters of correspondence, and additional diagrams, designs, photos, drawings, etc.)

Of course, since every science fair project is different, you may need to vary this format according to project type and the ways your experiment was conducted. This may be the case if you are writing a report for an engineering science project, which might have different report sections that discuss various designs and troubleshooting that took place.

The Abstract

An abstract is a brief project summary that is about a page in length. It explains the project's purpose and procedural plan and presents generalized data and a short discussion of your conclusions. Many local, state, and regional science fairs have made the abstract a mandatory part of the competition and require that it be completed and submitted to the science fair prior to the time you set up your exhibit. The abstract can serve as a record of what was conducted in connection with your project and might be printed in a book of abstracts from the fair. It also helps for placement in the correct scientific category of competition, and it helps the judges to quickly grasp the summary of your project. It may even suggest to the judges that they should consider your work for other awards sponsored by outside groups. One of the best ways to learn how to write an abstract is to read through lots of other students' abstracts. The sidebar shows an example.

ABSTRACT

The purpose of this project was to determine if dish towels contain bacteria after they have been used to dry dishes that have been handwashed, and if so, which type of dish towel harbors the most bacteria. It was hypothesized in comparing linen, cotton, and terry cloth dish towels that terry cloth dish towels would have the greatest amount of bacteria because of their thickness and absorbency, since linen and cotton dish towels have a tighter weave and thinner texture. Numerous experiments were conducted consisting of cultures taken from brand-new linen, cotton, and terry cloth dish towels that were used to dry cups and plates washed by hand with the same amount of liquid soap and water, at the same temperature and in the same environment. These tests were conducted thirty minutes, three hours, and three days after each towel had been used to determine and measure the presence of bacteria, if any, that were present in the towels. These test results were repeated on ten different occasions to obtain consistent data results. The results showed that both the linen and cotton dish towels had very little bacteria, while the terry cloth towels contained large amounts of bacteria in all test trials. Therefore, my hypothesis was correct: the existence and survival rate of bacteria was the greatest in the terry cloth towels.

The Backboard

The **backboard** is usually the most important part of your display, since it does the marketing and promoting of your science fair project. This is the first thing that viewers see. It has the power to gain a lot of attention for your project or just have viewers walk right past it. A well-done backboard should be your ultimate goal once you have your project report and abstract written.

The backboard should include all the major parts of your project. It is essentially an upright, self-supporting board with organized project highlights. It is usually three-sided, although it does not have to be. The backboard should meet the spacing standards of the Intel ISEF if you plan to enter a state or regional science fair affiliated with this organization. Since the dimensions of your display must not be more than 108 inches (274 centimeters) high, including the table, 30 inches (76 centimeters) deep, and 48 inches (122 centimeters) wide, your backboard must fit within these limits. If these dimensions are exceeded, you may be disqualified.

When constructing your backboard, stay away from thin posterboard or cardboard. Backboards made of these materials will bend and do not look very professional. Instead, purchase a firm, self-supporting material, such as a reinforced paperboard or corkboard. Alternatively, you may choose to purchase a premade backboard. In recent years, this has become a popular choice among students. Two companies that specialize in them are Showboard and Science Fair Supply. Both offer backboards in a variety of sizes and materials as well as other project display accessories. You can reach Showboard at 1-800-323-9189 or online at www.showboard.com. Science Fair Supply can be reached at 1-800-556-3247 or online at www.sciencefairsupply.com.

Select appropriate lettering for your backboard. Use your computer's word processor or purchase graphic design software that will help to make a neat, attractive presentation on your backboard. If you do not have software that will allow you to do this, you might want to purchase self-sticking letters. In recent years, almost all science fair project backboards at the state, regional, and international levels have typeface styles and background patterns that have been rendered in one of many terrific graphic design software programs. If you do not have such a program on your home computer, your school probably has one. Keep in mind that it is simply unacceptable to handprint your backboard, especially if you are aiming for a top-notch project.

Now that you know how to construct a backboard, you need to know what information you should put on it and where to place it. There is no standard way of making a backboard; however, all the information displayed on it should be well organized so that the concept of the project is easy to grasp. The project title, for example, should stand out in the middle section in bold print. The rest of your information should be placed in an orderly fashion from left to right under organized headings that follow the scientific method. You can also apply headings that relate more specifically to your subject. Make sure they are explicit so that a viewer can understand the purpose, hypothesis, objective, experimental plan, and data results quickly and efficiently.

The information you place under each heading is crucial. It must be concise and inclusive. Do not fill up your backboard with excessive fillers and distracting information. Try to summarize your statements under each heading in no more than three hundred words. Additional backboard space should be filled with helpful visual information on your subject.

— EXERCISE —

Now that you know what goes into a backboard, make a list of all the items you want to include on your own backboard. Write the information you will use under each of the main headings: purpose or problem, hypothesis, research, experimental plan, results, and conclusions. Choose the tables, graphs, diagrams, photos, and flow-charts that you are going to use. Pick out a computer-generated typeface style for your board and an appropriate color scheme. Use the following blank backboard panels to design the layout:

Plan the design and layout of your backboard using the following backboard panels. Use backboard subtitles (Purpose, Hypothesis, Research, Procedure, Results, Conclusion) on the backboard along with graphs, diagrams, photos, and drawings.

	Project Title	

Display Restrictions

The Intel ISEF and all of its affiliated science fairs have established strict regulations involving the exhibition of certain articles in conjunction with the rest of your exhibit. A summary follows of the Intel ISEF display and safety rules. If you have any questions, talk to your teacher or adviser, or contact your science fair administrator or Science Service, the organization that administers the Intel ISEF, for more information about what is acceptable for display. A rule of thumb is to avoid anything that could be potentially hazardous to display in public. The intent of the rule is to protect other students and the public. You can usually uphold such regulations by using photographs, drawings, graphs, charts, and model simulations (where permissible) to show the results of your investigation and research. If you have any doubts about displaying any part of your project, be sure to first check with officials from your local science fair or contact the Intel ISEF.

Items That Cannot Be Displayed

1. Live animals, living organisms, preserved vertebrate/invertebrate animals, taxidermy specimens or parts, including embryos.

2. All live materials, including plants and microbes.

3. Human or animal parts or body fluids (i.e., blood or urine) except teeth, hair, nails, histological dry mount sections and wet mount tissue slides properly acquired.

4. All soil and waste samples and related materials.

5. All chemicals, water, and their containers.

6. Poisons, drugs, controlled substances or hazardous substances or devices (e.g., firearms, weapons, ammunition).

7. Food, human or animal.

8. Syringes, pipettes, and similar devices and sharp objects.

9. Dry ice or other sublimating solids (e.g., solids that can vaporize into a gas without first becoming a liquid).

10. Any flames, open or concealed.

11. Highly flammable display materials.

12. Tanks that have contained combustible gases or liquids, unless purged with carbon dioxide.

13. Batteries with open-top cells.

14. Photographs and other visual presentations of surgical techniques, dissection, necropsies, and/or laboratory techniques depicting vertebrate animals in other-than-normal conditions.

15. Operation of Class III or IV lasers.

Items That Can Be Displayed with Restriction

1. Projects with unshielded belts, pulleys, chains, and moving parts with tension or pinch points.

2. Any device requiring voltage over 110 volts.

3. Soil or waste samples if permanently encased.

4. Empty tanks that previously contained combustible liquids or gases must be certified as having been purged with carbon dioxide.

5. Class III and IV lasers (but may not be operated).

6. Class II lasers containing a sign that reads "Laser Radiation—Do Not Stare into Beam," with a protective housing that prevents access to the beam, operated only during display, safety inspection, and judging.

7. Large vacuum tubes or dangerous ray-generating devices must be properly shielded.

8. Pressurized tanks that contained noncombustibles may be allowed if properly secured.

9. Any apparatus producing temperatures that will cause physical burns must be adequately shielded.

7
GETTING READY FOR THE FAIR

THE GAME PLAN

To be ready to attend the science fair, including setting up your project, and being prepared for oral presentation and judging.

Be sure to read all literature and information about science fair day or science fair week at the local, state, or regional science fair that you are attending so that you can make all necessary arrangements to arrive at the fair on time, have your project set up, and be present for oral presentation, judging, and award ceremonies. (You might just be a winner!) Many state and regional science fairs hold their oral presentation and judging sessions during normal school hours, so be sure to obtain a calendar of events so that you do not miss anything important and so that you can get permission for time off from school and transportation to and from the fair. You have just put in a great deal of work over the past several months researching, testing, and preparing your science fair project for this very occasion, so you don't want to miss out on any of it!

Setting Up Your Project

As you set up your project at the fair, pay careful attention to the space requirements mentioned in chapter 6 (the space should be marked off). Your backboard and display should already be self-supporting and ready to go, but it is wise to bring an

SCIENCE FAIR EMERGENCY KIT ITEMS

Here's a list of items to include in an emergency kit to bring to the science fair: spray mount, glue, stapler, masking tape or duct tape, scissors, pen, pencil, black marking pen, self-adhesive notes (for any important notes or last-minute instructions to judges concerning your display), screwdriver and extra screws (if your backboard contains hinges), extension cord (if applicable to your display), and extra copies of your project abstract (at least twenty-five copies should be placed in front of your backboard in a neat pile or a folder for use by judges, award sponsors, and the public).

emergency kit with you in case your backboard or display requires minor repairs or modifications by the time you get to the fair.

After your project is completely set up, a fair representative will check it to make sure everything complies with fair rules and safety regulations. Make sure that you have everything displayed properly and have any necessary instructions available for the fair staff or judges (this is especially important if you have a project that involves the use of a computer or some other type of mechanically operated display).

Judging at the State and Regional Fair Levels

At some fairs, judging takes place as soon as all the projects are set up. Students and parents are not allowed in the exhibit hall during this time. Generally, judges are assigned to separate divisions as teams. They begin by reviewing the projects in their category individually and then as a group, in which they exchange thoughts with team members and rank the projects. While judging systems vary, most state and regional fairs will typically spend one day on this type of preliminary judging where those projects that rank in the top 25 to 50 percent are determined and qualify to compete for the second round of judging, which is referred to as final judging. This final round determines place awards and eligibility of the best projects in grades 9 through 12 for the Intel ISEF.

During the final round of judging, state and regional science fair contestants who have made the first-round cut (finalists) are asked to come back to their projects and give an oral presentation for a variety of judges. These judges may represent the fair itself, professional and academic associations, or businesses that distribute specialized awards.

Most state and regional science fair judges score contestants on various criteria, including the following (terms in boldface are defined in the glossary).

1. *Scientific Approach to the Problem/ Engineering Goals:* This is often the most important and substantial criterion for judging. It measures whether the exhibitor shows evidence of applied scientific skill or engineering development through recognizing the scope and limitation of the issue that is being studied and the exhibitor's analysis in addressing the scope of the problem, including the quality of the work, time spent securing data on which observations have been based, and whether the observations support these data.

2. *Creative Ability/Originality:* This criterion also weighs substantially in the exhibitor's score and basically measures the ingenuity and originality of the problem that is being studied and/or the exhibitor's approach to the problem. Judges look for whether you have chosen the best method possible in your investigation and whether you have made the most effective use of materials, equipment, and techniques pertaining to your topic. This also takes into account whether your project is unique, how you derived your topic, and if credit is given to mentors who may have assisted you.

3. *Thoroughness and Accuracy:* This area measures the depth of the literature used concerning the project and the use and analysis of data results from the exhibitor's experiment, study, or investigation on which conclusions are based.

4. *Clarity:* This criterion determines whether the project's scope, purpose, or goals are clear and concise. Sometimes exhibitors get so swept away by the complexity of the subject and technicalities in their investigation that they lose sight of their basic goal and fail to communicate their project's purpose to the judges. While it is admirable to acquire a new scientific or technical lingo while studying and pursuing your topic, you will not impress anyone if you fail to communicate the topic clearly and concisely.

5. *Advancement of the Exhibitor's Knowledge in Science:* This area looks at whether the student has a good understanding of the primary aspects that concern his or her topic, including basic research and experimental principles, namely the control and handling of variables in experimentation, repeated trials, and the approach to reaching conclusions.

6. *Other:* Some science fairs also grade your exhibit partly on its dramatic value—that is, whether it is presented in a way that has visual appeal through the use of graphics and a clever or attractive layout. Also, to the extent that you may be working with a partner on a team science fair project, an additional part of your overall score may include points on how the project was handled by the team, project management, delegation and sharing of workload, expertise of each team member, and so on.

Keep in mind that judging is a difficult task that requires the skill and expertise of a wide range of qualified professionals. The judges are analyzing the overall quality of work that has been done on a subject that involved probing, testing, and reasoning in a creative sense. They are not interested in plain library research resembling a book report, meaningless collections, or work that was copied from books or someone else's science fair project.

Presenting Your Project in an Interview

If you make the cut and become a finalist, you will have the opportunity to be present with your project during judging, which is an enviable position. You will be able to explain in detail the purpose, research, experimental plan, procedures, methods, and conclusions in your project. Practice what you are going to say before the fair so that your presentation will be smooth and relaxed. If possible, have your mentor, teacher, or someone familiar with your project ask you key questions that are likely to be asked during judging.

Above all, the key is to be so well versed on your subject matter that you can handle random questions that come your way. Judges want to see that you understand your project thoroughly and that you actually did the work yourself. They do not want to hear a memorized presentation that sounds like you are reciting a script; they want to be able to interject and ask you questions so that they can see you are thinking on your feet. They want to understand exactly what you did and what you accomplished. If you cannot get these points across, you are not going to fare well, even if you conducted the most sophisticated experiment on the most interesting topic and achieved the most amazing results. None of this will matter if you do not communicate well to the judges. Be prepared to expertly handle questions.

Practice your responses to the following list of main questions that you will be expected to answer when you are presenting your project to a judge. Go over your responses several times so that you know them well. If possible, have your mentor, teacher, or someone familiar with your project pose these and any additional questions anticipated by the judges.

1. What is your project about?

2. Why did you select this project?

3. What did you expect to accomplish with your project?

4. Why did you choose the experiment that you did, and did it provide the answers to what you were seeking? (If not, be prepared to explain why.)

5. What was your experimental plan, how did you gather your data, and can you explain the data you obtained? (Be prepared to use your display as a visual aid. Also, if your experiment failed or if you cannot prove your hypothesis, be ready to explain what happened and what might have contributed to the results you obtained.)

6. Was this the best experiment to achieve your goal? (If it was not, be prepared to explain what could have been done differently.)

7. What conclusions have you drawn from this project, and what might be done to further your investigation in this project?

Every now and then, a judge will ask a question that no one could have anticipated, and you may not have the answer for it. Do not panic. Sometimes judges test you to see if you really did the work yourself and if you really have a handle on the subject matter. While you should be able to answer anything about your project that you have on your backboard and in your report or abstract, you might be surprised by this type of trick question. If you find yourself in this situation, just explain to the judge that because your project covered so many different aspects of the topic, you do not recall at the present time the answer to that particular question. You can also state that while you do not have the answer, you will certainly look into the question that was raised. Alternatively, offer the judge an explanation on something related to this line of questioning if you can, or just state that you are not familiar with the issue but that you would be glad to inform the judge about another aspect concerning the project that is extremely relevant to the results you achieved.

It is important to realize that science fair judges at the state and regional levels are typically experienced scientific researchers, engineers, mathematicians, doctors, and professors and are quite capable of detecting errors or fake experimental results. They will also be able to tell if you memorized your presentation or if someone else did the work for you. These individuals were selected as judges because they have a high level of expertise in a particular scientific discipline, which may incidentally be the category in which your project is entered at the fair. Also, be aware that the judge may have already seen a project similar to yours at another science fair.

Judging usually takes from a few hours to a full day with breakout sessions for lunch and workshops (at some fairs). Try to be consistent with every judge interviewing you; stay alert, and concentrate on what you want to say even though you may have already said the same thing to the last judge. If you must leave your project momentarily, post a note stating that you will return soon. Know your material, be thorough, be confident, communicate well, and enjoy a wonderful experience!

Specialized Awards

There are special areas of competition at some science fairs that are separate from the general fair honors. These special categories are accessible to students who complete a project concentrated in a particular area of science. Various companies and organizations present awards to honor excellence in a subject area related to their organization's specialized field. These awards sometimes consist of prestigious scholarships, grants, and internships.

Congratulations!

Be sure to congratulate yourself and your colleagues for a job well done. A science fair project is no small task, and making it to a science fair is an incredible achievement that you should be proud of. Science fairs are exciting and fun, providing rewarding opportunities to learn new skills and make new friends. I hope you have found that your project was not only a great learning experience but enjoyable as well. Hats off to you!

Appendix A

(SI) METRIC AND ENGLISH CONVERSION TABLES

Use these tables to convert measurements between the English and (SI) metric systems.

Length

English	Symbol	(SI) Metric	Symbol
I inch	in.	2.54 centimeters	cm
I foot	ft.	30.40 centimeters	cm
I yard	yd.	0.90 meter	m
I mile	mi.	1.60 kilometers	km

(SI) Metric	Symbol	English	Symbol
I centimeter	cm = 10 mm	0.3937 inches	in.
I meter	m = 100 cm	1.0936 yards	yd.
I kilometer	km = 1,000 m	0.6214 miles	mi.

Multiply the English measurement by the multiplier in the far right column to come up with the metric equivalent.

English	To Metric	Multiplier
inches	centimeters	2.54
feet	centimeters	30.5
yards	meters	0.914
miles	kilometers	1.61

Weight (Mass)

English	Symbol	(SI) Metric	Symbol
I ounce	oz.	28.34 grams	g
I pound	lb. = 16 ounces	0.45 kilograms	kg
I ton	lb. = 2,240 pounds	1.0161 metric tons	t

Weight (Mass) (continued)

(SI) Metric	Symbol	English	Symbol
1 milligram	mg = 1,000 mcg	0.0000353 ounces	oz.
1 gram	g = 1,000 mg	0.0352739 ounces	oz.
1 kilogram	kg = 1,000 g	2.2046224 pounds	lb.
1 metric ton	t = 1,000 kg	1.1023113 tons	t

Multiply the English measurement by the multiplier in the far right column to come up with the metric equivalent.

English	To Metric	Multiplier
ounces	grams	28.3
pounds	kilograms	0.45

Volume

English	Symbol	(SI) Metric	Symbol
1 teaspoon	tsp.	4.92 milliliters	ml
1 tablespoon	tbsp.	14.78 milliliters	ml
1 fluid ounce	fl. oz.	29.57 milliliters	ml
1 cup	c. = 8 fl. oz.	0.24 liters	l
1 pint	pt. = 16 fl. oz.	0.47 liters	l
1 quart	qt. = 32 fl. oz.	0.95 liters	l
1 gallon	gal. = 128 fl oz.	3.79 liters	l

(SI) Metric	Symbol	English	Symbol
1 milliliter	ml = 1,000 mcl	0.0338140 fluid ounces	fl. oz.
1 liter	l = 1,000 ml	33.814022 fluid ounces	fl. oz.

Multiply the English measurement by the multiplier in the far right column to come up with the metric equivalent.

English	To Metric	Multiplier
teaspoons	milliliters	5
cups	milliliters	250
quarts	liters	0.95

Temperature

Water freezes at: 32 degrees Fahrenheit or 32°F   0 degrees Celsius or 0°C

Water boils at: 212 degrees Fahrenheit or 212°F   100 degrees Celsius or 100°C

Normal human body temperature: 98.6 degrees Fahrenheit   37 degrees Celsius or 37°C

To convert Fahrenheit to Celsius:

$(°F - 32) \times \frac{5}{9}$

To convert Celsius to Fahrenheit:

$$\frac{°C}{\frac{5}{9}} + 32$$

Conversion Calculations for My Project:

Appendix B

SCIENTIFIC SUPPLY COMPANIES

You can obtain laboratory and other scientific supplies and instruments from these companies. They were selected because they specialize in equipment geared to science fair projects or equipment that is normally used in a school laboratory.

Northeast and Atlantic

Auspex Scientific
1416 Union Blvd.
Allentown, PA 18109
(610) 776-1888
www.aupexscientifc.com

Connecticut Valley Biological Supply Co.
82 Valley Rd.
P.O. Box 326
Southampton, MA 01703
(413) 527-4030
(800) 628-7748
www.ctvalleybio.com

Edmund Scientific Co.
60 Pearce Ave.
Tonawanda, NY 14150-6711
(800) 728-6999
www.scientificsonline.com

MiniScience.Com
1059 Main Ave.
Clifton, NJ 07011
(973) 777-3113
www.miniscience.com

The Science Fair, Inc.
140 College Square
Newark, DE 19711-5447
(302) 453-1817
www.thesciencefair.com

Science Kit and Boreal Labs
777 E. Park Dr.
P.O. Box 5003
Tonawanda, NY 14150
(800) 828-7777
www.sciencekit.com

Thomas Scientific
99 High Hill Rd.
Swedesboro, NJ 08085
(856) 467-2000
(800) 345-2100
www.thomassci.com

Ward's Natural Science
P.O. Box 92912
Rochester, NY 14692-9012
(800) 962-2660
www.wardsci.com

Southeast

Advance Scientific & Chemical, Inc.
2345 S.W. 34th St.
Fort Lauderdale, FL 33312
(800) 524-2436
www.advance-scientific.com

Carolina Biological Supply Co.
2700 York Rd.
Burlington, NC 27215-3398
(800) 334-5551
www.carolina.com

Kenin Scientific Discount
1830 N.E. 163 St.
North Miami Beach, FL 33312
(305) 940-7804
(800) 600-6291
www.kenin.com

Midwest

American Science & Surplus
5316 N. Milwaukee Ave.
Chicago, IL 60630
(847) 647-0011
(773) 763-0313
www.sciplus.com

BME Lab Store
2459 University Ave., W.
St. Paul, MN 55114
(651) 646-5339

Fisher Science Education
4500 Turnberry
Hanover Park, IL 60133
(800) 955-1177
www.fisheredu.com

Frey Scientific Co.
100 Paragon Parkway
Manfield, OH 44903
(800) 225-3739
www.freyscientific.com

Sargent-Welch
7300 N. Linden Ave.
P.O. Box 5229
Buffalo Grove, IL 60089-5229
(800) 727-4368
www.sargentwelch.com

South Central

Capitol Scientific, Inc.
2500 Rutland St.
Austin, TX 78766
(512) 836-1167

NASCO
901 Janesville Ave.
Fort Atkinson, WI 53538
(800) 558-9595
www.enasco.com

Sciencelab.com
1407 N. Park Drive
Kingwood, TX 77339
(281) 354-6400
www.sciencelab.com

Science Stuff
7801 N. Lamar Blvd.
Suite E-190
Austin, TX 78752-1016
(800) 795-7315
www.sciencestuff.com

West

All World Scientific
5515 186 Place S.W.
Lynnwood, WA 98037
(425) 672-4228
(800) 28-WORLD
www.awscientific.com

Amico Scientific
1161 Cushman Ave.
San Diego, CA 92110
(619) 543-9200

A. Warren's Educational Supplies
980 W. San Bernardino Rd.
Covina, CA 91722
(626) 966-1731
www.warrenseducational.com

Hawaii Chemical & Scientific
2363 North King St.
Honolulu, HI 96819-3616
(800) 841-4265
www.hawaiiscientific.com

Tri-Ess Sciences
1020 Chestnut St.
Burbank, CA 91506
(818) 848-7838 (inside California)
(800) 274-6910 (outside California)
www.tri-esssciences.com

Canada

Northwest Scientific Supply
P.O. Box 6100 #301-3060
Cedar Hill Rd.
Victoria, B.C. V8T 3J5
Canada
(250) 592-2438
www.nwscience.com

Appendix C

SAMPLE PROJECT JOURNAL PAGES AND WORKSHEETS

Duplicate the layout of the following pages in organizing your project journal so that information can be easily recorded and retrieved for future reference.

Journal Sample A

Project Progress Outline and Checklist:

I. Find Science Project Topic   _____
    A. Conduct initial reading research about topic and learn
       what is generally known about it.   _____
    B. Consult with science teacher/adviser to find out if
       project idea is feasible and permissible, and whether
       strict guidelines apply to your subject matter.   _____
        i. If strict guidelines apply, find out what you can do with
           your subject matter, who you need to work with, and
           all permission forms that need to be completed prior
           to starting your research.   _____
        ii. Obtain all the forms, find any specialist you need to
           work with, and complete all forms by project
           submission deadline (usually November or
           December).   _____

II. Conduct More Serious Research About Topic   _____
    A. Perform more research of articles and literature.   _____
    B. Identify and make contact with key resources found
       through articles and literature, referrals, networking, etc.   _____
        i. Make contact with key resources via telephone call
           or written letter or e-mail to request help, advice,
           and suggestions.   _____
        ii. Try to secure a mentor.   _____

III. Develop Your Research Plan   _____
    A. State your hypothesis in a meaningful way.   _____
    B. State your project objective.   _____
    C. Create an experimental procedural plan.   _____
        i. Identify the best experiment to provide the answers
           to the question you are researching or to achieve
           your goal.   _____
        ii. Determine variables and controls and how you will
           gather data.   _____
        iii. Identify all materials, supplies, equipment, test
           subjects, and testing facilities needed; skills and
           techniques to be learned; and assistance needed
           to carry out the experiment.   _____
        iv. Determine how safety precautions and procedures
           will be instituted under research guidelines.   _____
    D. Submit research plan to science teacher or adviser along
       with all completed forms for final approval.   _____

IV. Conduct Experiment   _____

    A. Set up and organize experiment.   _____

    B. Collect data.   _____

    C. Record data.   _____

    D. Analyze data through tables, diagrams, charts, and
statistical analysis.   _____

V. Finalize Project   _____

    A. Write project report and abstract.   _____

    B. Build backboard for project display.   _____

    C. Follow display rules and guidelines.   _____

    D. Prepare for oral presentation and science fair
judging questions.   _____

Journal Sample B

Daily Entry

Date:

What I worked on today:

_____

_____

_____

_____

_____

_____

_____

Correspondence made, meetings attended, places I visited:

_____

_____

_____

_____

_____

_____

_____

Experimental procedures made and observations noted:

_____

_____

_____

_____

_____

_____

_____

_____

_____

_____

_____

_____

_____

_____

_____

_____

What I learned today (facts, techniques, procedures, methods, conclusions, etc.):

_____

_____

_____

_____

_____

_____

_____

_____

_____

_____

_____

_____

Journal Sample C

Information Read and Used for My Science Project Topic

1. Name of Article: _____ Author: _____

Publication (Source): _____ Year: _____

Date Found: _____ Date Read: _____

Article Summary:

_____

_____

_____

_____

2. Name of Article: _____ Author: _____

Publication (Source): _____ Year: _____

Date Found: _____ Date Read: _____

Article Summary:

_____

_____

_____

_____

3. Name of Article: _____ Author: _____

Publication (Source): _____ Year: _____

Date Found: _____ Date Read: _____

Article Summary:

_____

_____

_____

_____

4. Name of Article: _____ Author: _____

Publication (Source): _____ Year: _____

Date Found: _____ Date Read: _____

Article Summary:

_____

_____

_____

_____

5. Name of Article: _____ Author: _____

Publication (Source): _____ Year: _____

Date Found: _____ Date Read: _____

Article Summary:

_____

_____

_____

_____

Journal Sample D

Science Project Contacts

Name: _____

Title: _____

Place of Business: _____

Department: _____

Address:

_____

_____

Telephone Number: _____

Fax Number: _____

E-mail Addresses: _____

Web Site Address: _____

Date I attempted to make contact: _____

I attempted contact with this party by: formal letter _____ telephone _____
e-mail _____

I received a response and/or was able to speak with this person: yes _____
no _____

(If no) I made another attempt to contact this party on: _____(date)

I made my second attempt to contact by: formal letter _____ telephone _____
e-mail _____

I received a response on my second attempt and/or was able to speak with this person: yes _____ no _____

(If a response was received):

Information, guidance, or advice I received from this contact:

_____

_____

_____

_____

_____

_____

_____

_____

_____

Referrals I received from this contact:

_____

_____

_____

_____

_____

_____

_____

_____

Books, articles, materials, or equipment I was given/loaned from this contact. (Be sure to log in any written materials in the "Information Read and Used on My Project Topic" section of your journal):

_____

_____

_____

_____

_____

_____

_____

_____

Journal Sample E

Worksheet for Materials and Facilities Needed: Supplies, Equipment, and Test Subjects Bought, Donated, or Loaned; or Facilities Donated

Laboratory supplies and equipment (petri dishes, test tubes, pipettes, beakers, thermometers, etc., and computers, incubators, microscopes, spectrophotometers, telescopes, and other devices, etc.):

Type of material:

_____

This material is being: bought _____ donated _____ loaned _____

This material is being procured from:

_____

Use of this material will be: at home _____ school _____ other facility _____

If "other," state where you are working with this material, the name of the party whose supervision you are under, and the arrangement or relationship you have with this facility and party:

_____

_____

_____

_____

What is this material used for in your project?:

_____

_____

_____

Is special training, supervision, or permission necessary to use this material?: yes _____ no _____

If "yes," how are you being trained to use this material and who is training or working with you in the use of this material?:

_____

_____

_____

_____

_____

_____

_____

For test subjects (humans, animals, plants; human, plant, and animal tissues, recombinant DNA, microbial cultures, pathogenic materials, chemicals, controlled substances, hazardous substances or devices):

Type of subject matter:

_____

Humans

_____ If subject matter comprises humans, approval obtained by Institutional Review Board (IRB) (check when completed).

Animals, plants; human, plant and animal tissues, recombinant DNA, microbial cultures, pathogenic materials, chemicals, controlled substances, hazardous substances or devices

_____ Proper and legal procurement and care of subject matter complies with local, state, or regional science fair and all applicable laws (check when completed)

This subject matter is being: bought _____ donated _____ loaned _____

Use of this subject matter will be at:

_____

Experimentation of subject matter will be overseen by the following qualified scientist/designated supervisor:

_____

_____

All necessary forms obtained and properly filled out (check when completed) _____

Appendix D

SAMPLE SCIENCE FAIR PROJECT FORMS

The following forms have been reproduced with permission from the most recent *International Rules for Precollege Science Research and Guidelines for Science and Engineering Fairs* booklet that is published annually by Science Service of Washington, D.C. These forms are the actual forms used by contestants competing in the Intel International Science and Engineering Fair and are similar to forms used by local, state, and regional science fair affiliates. They are reprinted here to give you an idea of the information requested on these forms. The forms process has become an integral and critical part of working on a science fair project and submitting it for competition at a science fair. Remember to check with your local, state, or regional science fair and/or mentor for the appropriate forms that apply to you.

Checklist for Adult Sponsor / Safety Assessment Form (1)
This completed form is required for ALL projects and must be completed prior to experimentation

Student's Name _____

1) ☐ The student and a parent / guardian have signed the **Approval Form (1B)**.

2) ☐ I have reviewed the **Research Plan (1A), Research Plan Attachment** and signed **Approval Form (1B)**.

3) ☐ This project involves the following area(s) and requires **SRC/IRB approval** before experimentation begins:

☐ **Human Subjects**   ☐ **Controlled Substances**

☐ **Vertebrate Animals**   ☐ **Recombinant DNA**

☐ **Pathogenic Agents***

   * All bacteria, fungi, etc. isolated from the environment should be considered potentially pathogenic.

4) ☐ This project does not involve any of the research areas listed in #3.

5) ☐ This project involves human subjects. The student will obtain approval from an **Institutional Review Board (IRB)** before experimentation is started. (See pp. 12-14.)

6) ☐ This project involves vertebrate animals, pathogenic agents, controlled substances or recombinant DNA. The student will obtain approval from a **Scientific Review Committee (SRC)/IACUC** before experimentation is started. (See pp. 15-23.)

7) ☐ This project involves tissues or the use of hazardous substances or devices checked below. A Designated Supervisor will provide proper supervision to the student. Prior approval by the adult sponsor and certification by a designated supervisor is required. (See p. 19, p. 23.)

☐ **Tissues** I have reviewed with the student the research plan and determined that this project is a tissue study and that, if applicable, the tissue was obtained from an animal sacrified for a purpose other than the student's project.

☐ **Chemicals** (*i.e.*, hazardous, flammable, explosive or highly toxic; carcinogens; mutagens and all pesticides). I have reviewed with the student the Material Safety Data Sheet (MSDS) Listing for each chemical that will be used. I have also reviewed the proper safety standards for each chemical including toxicity data, proper handling techniques, and disposal methods. For *Safety in Academic Chemistry Laboratories*, visit the American Chemical Society's website at http://pubs.acs.org.

☐ **Equipment** (*i.e.*, welders; lasers; voltage greater than 220 volts). I have reviewed with the student the proper operational procedures and safety precautions for the equipment to be used by the student. For information about laser standards and research, visit the OSHA website at www.osha.gov.

☐ **Firearms**. I have reviewed with the student the proper safety standards for firearms use.

☐ **Radioactive Substances**. I have reviewed the proper safety standards for each radioactive substance the student will use.

☐ **Radiation** (*i.e.*, x-ray or nuclear; unshielded ionizing radiation of 100-400 nm wavelength). I have reviewed with the student the proper safety methods concerning the type of radiation the student will use.

_____   _____   _____

Adult Sponsor's Printed Name   Signature   Date of Review
                                                                                     (Must be prior to experimentation.)

Research Plan (1A)

This completed form is required for ALL projects.
Type or print all information requested.
Answer all questions and complete Research Plan Attachment (see page 28)

1) Student's Name _____ Grade _____

2) Title of Project _____

_____

3) Adult Sponsor _____ Phone:_____ Email: _____

4) Is this a continuation from a previous year? ☐ Yes ☐ No

    If Yes: a) Attach the previous year's **abstract, Research Plan 1A and Research Plan Attachment** and

            b) Explain how this project is new and different from previous years on **Continuation Form (7)**

5) **This year's** laboratory experiment/data collection will begin: **(must be stated (mm/dd/yy)**

     Projected Start Date: _____   Projected End Date: _____

     ACTUAL Start Date:_____   ACTUAL End Date: _____

6) Where will you conduct your lab work? (check all that apply) ☐ Research Institution ☐ School ☐ Field ☐ Home

7) Name, address & phone of school and work site(s):

     School: Work site: Work site:

---

8)   **All projects require completed forms: Checklist for Adult Sponsor/Safety Assessment Form (1), Research Plan (1A), Research Plan Attachment and Approval Form (1B) and may require Regulated Research Institutional/Industrial Setting Form (1C).**

     Check **ALL** items that apply to your research.

     The following areas require review and approval by SRC or IRB prior to experimentation :

     ☐ **Humans** (requires prior IRB approval; complete Forms: Checklist, 1A, 1B, 4 [1C, 2, 3, if required]

     ☐ **Vertebrate Animals** (requires prior SRC or IACUC approval, complete: Checklist, 1A, 1B, 5A or 5B [1C, 2, 3, if required])

     ☐ **Pathogens** (requires prior SRC approval; complete Forms: Checklist, 1A, 1B, 2 [1C, 3, if required])

     ☐ **Controlled Substances** (requires prior SRC approval; complete Forms: Checklist, 1A, 1B, 2 or 3 [1C, 2, 3 as required])

     ☐ **Recombinant DNA** (requires prior SRC approval, complete Forms: Checklist, 1A, 1B [2, 3, 1C, as required])

     The following areas require approval by a Designated Supervisor prior to experimentation:

     ☐ **Human/Animal Tissue** (complete Forms: Checklist, 1A, 1B, 3, 6 [1C, if required])

     ☐ **Hazardous Substances or Devices** (complete Forms: Checklist, 1A, 1B, 3 [1C, if required])

9) **Complete Research Plan Attachment (See page 28) and attach to this form.**

10) **An abstract is required for all projects after experimentation (see page 24).**

International Rules 2004/2005   full text of the rules and electronic copies of forms are available at www.sciserv.org/isef   Page 27

111

Research Plan Attachment
REQUIRED for ALL Projects
A complete research plan must accompany Research Plan Form (1A)
Additional pages may be attached

Student Name(s): _____

Provide a typed research plan and attach to Research Plan Form (1A).

The research plan is to include the following:

A. Question being addressed

B. Hypothesis/Problem/Engineering Goals

C. Description in detail of method or procedures (including chemical concentrations and drug dosages)

For human research, include survey or questionnaires if used, and critically evaluate the risk. See instructions for human research on p. 12 of the Rules. **For vertebrate animal research, you must briefly discuss POTENTIAL ALTERNATIVES and present a detailed justification for use of vertebrate animals**. See instructions on p. 15 of the International Rules.

D. Bibliography

List at least five major references (*e.g.*, science journal articles, books, internet sites) from your library research.

If you plan to use vertebrate animals, give an additional animal care reference.

Approval Form (1B)
This completed form is required for ALL projects.

1) REQUIRED FOR ALL PROJECTS.

a) Student Acknowledgment: I understand the risks and possible dangers to me of the proposed **Research Plan (1A)**. I will adhere to all International Rules when conducting this research.

Student's Printed Name	Signature	Date Acknowledged
		(Must be prior to experimentation.)

b) Parent/Guardian Approval: I have read and understand the risks and possible dangers involved in the **Research Plan (1A)** and **Attachment**. I consent to my child participating in this research.

Parent/Guardian's Printed Name	Signature	Date of Approval
		(Must be prior to experimentation.)

c) Adult Sponsor Approval: I have read the **Research Plan (1A)** and **Attachment** prior to experimentation and reviewed the **Checklist for Adult Sponsor** with the student. I agree to sponsor the student named above and assume reasonable responsibility for compliance with all International ISEF Rules as they pertain to the **Research Plan (1A)**.

Adult Sponsor's Printed Name	Signature	Date of Approval
		(Must be prior to experimentation.)

2) REQUIRED FOR PROJECTS REQUIRING SRC/IRB APPROVAL. SIGN 2a OR 2b AS APPROPRIATE.

a) Required for projects that need prior SRC/IRB approval BEFORE experimentation (i.e., see Item #8 on Form 1A.)

The SRC/IRB has carefully studied this project's **Research Plan (1A) and Attachment** and all the required forms are included. My signature indicates approval of the **Research Plan (1A)** before the student begins experimentation.

SRC/IRB Chair's Printed Name

Signature   Date of Approval
(Must be prior to experimentation.)

OR

b) Required for research conducted at all Regulated Research Institutions with no prior fair SRC/IRB approval.

This project was conducted at a regulated research institution (**not home or high school, etc.**), was reviewed and approved by the proper institutional board before experimentation and complies with the ISEF Rules. **Attach (1C) and required institutional approvals (e.g. IACUC, IRB)**

SRC/IRB Chair's Printed Name

Signature   Date of Approval

NOTE: If a stamp is used, it <u>must</u> be initialed by the chairperson.

3) FINAL ISEF AFFILIATED FAIR SRC APPROVAL. (REQUIRED FOR ALL PROJECTS)

SRC Approval After Experimentation and Shortly Before Competition at Regional/State/National Fair
I certify that this project adheres to the approved **Research Plan (1A)** and **Attachment** and complies with all ISEF Rules.

Regional SRC Chair's Printed Name	Signature	Date of Approval
State/National SRC Chair's Printed Name *(where applicable)*	Signature	Date of Approval

Regulated Research Institutional/Industrial Setting Form (1C)

This form must be completed by the scientist supervising the student research conducted in a regulated research institution (*e.g.*, universities, medical centers, NIH, etc.) or industrial setting.

This form MUST be displayed with your project.

Student's Name _____

Title of Project _____

To be completed by the Scientist (NOT the Student or Adult Sponsor) after experimentation:

The student conducted research at my institution: (check one)

a) ☐ only to use the equipment   b) ☐ to perform experiment(s)

If b, the following questions must be answered.

1) <u>How did the student get the idea for her/his project?</u>
   (e.g. Was the project assigned, picked from a list, an original student idea, etc.)

2) <u>Were you made aware of the ISEF rules before experimentation?</u>   ☐ Yes   ☐ No

3) <u>Did the student work on the project as a part of a research group?</u>   ☐ Yes   ☐ No
   If yes, how large was the group and what kind of research group was it (students, group of adult researchers, etc.)

4) <u>What specific procedures did the student actually perform and how independently did the student work?</u>
   Please list and describe. (Do not list procedures student **only** observed.)

Student research projects dealing with human subjects, vertebrate animals or rDNA require review and approval by an institutional regulatory board (IRB/IACUC). **Copy of approval(s) must be attached.**

Scientist's Printed Name _____   Signature _____   Title _____

Institution _____   Date Signed _____

Address _____   Email/ Phone _____

Qualified Scientist Form (2)

Required for research involving pathogens; may be required for research involving rDNA, vertebrate animals, controlled substances and humans. Must be signed prior to the start of student experimentation.

Student's Name _____

Title of Project _____

To be completed by the Qualified Scientist (qualifications must be in student's area of research):

Scientist's Name _____

<u>Advanced</u> Degree _____ Degree Specialty (must be stated) _____

If degree does not clarify qualifications in student's area of research, please explain:

_____

Position: _____ Institution: _____

Address: _____ Email/Phone: _____

1) Will vertebrate animals be used? . . . . ☐ yes ☐ no

   a) If yes, were alternatives (see page 15) explored? . . . . ☐ yes ☐ no

   b) Could this project cause pain or distress to the vertebrate animal(s)? . . . . ☐ yes ☐ no

   c) Does this project duplicate previously published research? . . . . ☐ yes ☐ no

   If yes to any of the above (a, b, c) please explain and justify: _____

_____

2) Will human subjects be used? . . . . ☐ yes ☐ no

3) Will controlled substances be used? . . . . ☐ yes ☐ no

   (includes DEA classed substances, prescription drugs, alcohol and tobacco)

   If yes, a) Will they be used according to existing local, state and

            federal regulations? . . . . ☐ yes ☐ no

       b) Please list the name(s) of the controlled substance(s): _____

4) Will recombinant DNA be used? . . . . ☐ yes ☐ no

5) Will pathogenic or potentially pathogenic agents be used? . . . . ☐ yes ☐ no

   If yes, name(s) _____

   If yes, will accepted procedures be used? . . . . ☐ yes ☐ no

6) Will tissues or body fluids be used? . . . . ☐ yes ☐ no

7) Will hazardous substances be used? . . . . ☐ yes ☐ no

8) Will you directly supervise the student(s)? . . . . ☐ yes ☐ no

   If yes, please explain what safety precautions will be taken in this study: _____

_____

I certify that I have reviewed and approved the **Research Plan (1A)** and **Attachment** prior to the start of the experimentation. If the student or Designated Supervisor is not trained in the necessary procedures, I will ensure her/his training. I will provide advice and supervision during the research. I have a working knowledge of the techniques to be used by the student in the **Research Plan (1A)** and **Attachment**. If an addictive substance is used in this research, I certify that I possess a DEA license required for procuring and dispensing an addictive substance. I understand that a Designated Supervisor is required when the student is not conducting experimentation under my direct supervision.

_____   _____   _____

Qualified Scientist's Printed Name   Signature   Date of Approval

                                           (Must be prior to experimentation.)

Human Subjects Form (4)
Required for all research involving humans. IRB approval required before experimentation.

Student's Name _____

Title of Project _____

To be completed by Student Researcher: (All questions are applicable and must be answered; additional page may be attached.)

1) Describe the purpose of this study and list all of the research procedures in which the subject will be involved. Include the duration of the subject's involvement. Attach any survey or questionnaire.

2) Describe and assess any potential risk or discomfort, and, if any, potential benefits (physical, psychological, social, legal or other) that may be reasonably expected by participating in this research.

3) Describe the procedures that will be used to minimize risk, to obtain informed consent, and to maintain confidentiality.

For questions or concerns regarding this research, contact: _____ at _____.
                                                                 Adult Sponsor   Email/phone

---

To be completed by Institutional Review Board (IRB) prior to experimentation: Determination of risk, including physical and psychological risks (See risk evaluation, p. 12.)

☐ **Minimal risk where informed consent is recommended, but not required.**
Justification for waiver of informed consent for research with survey of subjects under the age of 18: _____

☐ **Minimal risk where informed consent is REQUIRED.**

☐ **More than minimal risk where informed consent & a Qualified Scientist are REQUIRED**

IRB SIGNATURES (a minimum of three signatures is required)

1) **Medical Professional:** *(circle)* (a licensed psychologist, psychiatrist, medical doctor, licensed social worker, physician's assistant, or registered nurse)

Member of IRB's Printed Name	Signature	Date of Approval

2) **Science Teacher:**

Member of IRB's Printed Name	Signature	Date of Approval

3) **School Administrator:**

Member of IRB's Printed Name	Signature	Date of Approval

To be completed by Human Subject:	**To be completed by Parent/Guardian:**
(prior to experimentation)	(Prior to experimentation and when participant is under 18 and informed consent is required)
☐ I have read and understand the conditions and risks above and I consent/assent to voluntarily participate in this research study.	☐ I have read and understand the conditions and risks above and consent to the participation of my child.
☐ I realize I am free to withdraw my consent and to withdraw from this study at any time without negative consequences.	☐ I have reviewed a copy of any survey or questionnaire used in the research.
☐ I consent to the use of visual images (photos, videos, etc.) involving my participation in this research.	☐ I consent to the use of visual images (photos, videos, etc.) involving my child in this research.
Signature _____ Date _____	Signature _____ Date _____

International Rules 2004/2005 full text of the rules and electronic copies of forms are available at www.sciserv.org/isef   Page 34

116

Vertebrate Animal Form (5A)
Required for all research involving vertebrate animals that is conducted in a Non-Regulated Research Site. (SRC approval required before experimentation.)

Student's Name _____

Title of Project _____

To be completed by Student Researcher:

1. Common name (or Genus, species) and number of animals used.

2. Describe completely the housing and husbandry to be provided. Include the cage/pen size, number of animals per cage, environment, bedding, type of food, frequency of food and water, how often animal is observed, etc.

3. What will happen to the animals after experimentation?

To be completed by Scientific Review Committee (SRC) PRIOR to experimentation:

☐ Observational study only. Veterinarian and Designated Supervisor NOT required.

☐ Behavioral or nutritional study. Designated Supervisor REQUIRED. Please have applicable person sign below.

☐ Behavioral or nutritional study. Veterinarian and Designated Supervisor REQUIRED. Please have applicable persons sign below.

☐ Behavioral or nutritional study. Veterinarian, Designated Supervisor and Qualified Scientist REQUIRED. Please have applicable persons sign below and complete a Qualified Scientist Form (2).

The SRC has carefully reviewed this study and finds it is an appropriate study and may be conducted in a non-regulated research site.

SRC Pre-Approval Signature:

_____   _____   _____
SRC Chair Printed Name   Signature   Date of Approval

To be completed by Veterinarian:

☐ I certify that I have reviewed this research and animal husbandry with the student prior to the start of experimentation.

☐ I certify that I will provide veterinary medical and nursing care in case of illness or emergency.

_____   _____
Printed Name   Email/Phone

_____   _____
Signature   Date of Approval

To be completed by Designated Supervisor:

I certify that I have reviewed this research and animal husbandry with the student prior to the start of experimentation and I accept primary responsibility for the quality of care and handling of the animals in this project.

☐ Additionally, I certify that I will directly supervise the experiment.

_____   _____
Printed Name   Email/Phone

_____   _____
Signature   Date of Approval

Vertebrate Animal Form (5B)

Required for all research involving vertebrate animals that is conducted at a Regulated Research Institution. (IACUC approval required before experimentation.)

Student's Name _____

Title of Project _____

Title and Protocol Number of IACUC Approved Project _____

_____

To be completed by Qualified Scientist or Principal Investigator:

1. Was this a student-generated idea or was it a subset of your work?

2. Were you made aware of the ISEF Rules before the student began experimentation?

3. What laboratory training, including dates, was provided to the student?

4. Species of animals used: _____ Number of animals used: _____

5. USDA Pain Category designated for this study:

6. Describe, in detail, the role of the student in this project: procedures and equipment they were involved with, oversight provided and safety precautions employed. (Attach extra pages if necessary.)

7. **Attach a copy of the Regulated Research Institution IACUC Approval.** A letter from the Qualified Scientist or Principal Investigator is not sufficient.

Certification or Documentation of Student Researcher Training

_____   _____

List Certificate Number or Attach Documentation   Date(s) of Training

_____   _____   _____

QS/PI Printed Name   Signature   Date

_____   _____   _____

IACUC Chair/Coordinator Printed Name   Signature   Date

Human and Vertebrate Animal Tissue Form (6)

Required for all projects using fresh tissue, organs, primary cell cultures, established cell and tissue cultures, meat or meat by-products, human or animal parts, including blood, blood products, teeth and body fluids.

If the research involves living organisms, please ensure that the proper human or animal forms are completed.

Student's Name _____

Title of Project _____

To be completed by Student Researcher:

1) What tissue(s), organ(s), or part(s) will be used?

2) Where will the above tissue, organ, or part be obtained (identify each separately):

3) If the tissue is obtained from a source within a research institution, please provide information regarding the vertebrate study from which the tissue was obtained. Include the name of the research institution, the title of the study, the IACUC approval number and date of IACUC approval.

To be completed by the Designated Supervisor:

☐ I verify that the student will work solely with organs, tissues, cultures or cells that will be supplied to him/her by myself or qualified personnel from the laboratory; and that if vertebrate animals were euthanized they were euthanized for a purpose other than the student's research.

AND/OR

☐ I certify that the blood, blood products, tissues or body fluids in this project will be handled in accordance with the standards and guidance set forth in Occupational Safety and Health Act, 29CFR, Subpart Z, 1910.1030 - <u>Blood Borne Pathogens</u>.

_____   _____   _____
Printed Name   Signature   Date Signed
                                                                                        (Must be prior to experimentation.)

_____   _____
Title   Phone

_____
Institution

International Rules 2004/2005   **full text of the rules and electronic copies of forms are available at www.sciserv.org/isef**   Page 37

119

GLOSSARY

abstract A brief summary of a science fair project (approximately three hundred words) that explains the project's objective and procedure and provides generalized data and a workable solution to the problem addressed by the subject.

backboard A self-supporting bulletin board (usually three-sided) that contains a summary outline of a science project. The backboard contains the project title and topic progression, together with flowcharts, photographs, and other significant project descriptions. The information on a backboard is usually organized according to the steps of the scientific method.

clarity A judging criterion that determines whether a project's scope, purpose, or goals are clear and concise.

conclusion The solution to a proposed issue or question, and confirmation or rejection of a hypothesis.

control A part of an experiment that is identical to the experimental group but is not altered, changed, or varied. It provides a guideline for comparing the experimental group.

creative ability An important judging criterion that determines ingenuity and originality of the problem being studied and/or the exhibitor's approach to the problem.

data Recorded information that is organized for final analysis and observation.

dependent variable The aspect of an experiment that is being measured; it is influenced by the independent variable.

Discovery Channel Young Scientist Challenge (DCYSC) Since 1999, this science fair, administered by Science Service, has been held for the top science fair projects for students in grades 5 through 8.

display The complete setup of a science fair project. It includes a backboard, a representation of the subject matter or experimental results, and a research report.

Empirical Rule (sometimes referred to as the 68-95-99.7 Rule) This rule represents the dynamic of a bell-shaped curve where there is an even distribution of data from the center of the curve with 68 percent of the data lying one standard deviation away from the mean in both directions, 95 percent of the data lying two standard deviations away from the mean in both directions, and 99.7 percent of the data lying three standard deviations away from the mean in both directions.

erroneous hypothesis An incorrect or vague hypothesis that does not support the experimental results.

experiment The part of a science project where a series of tests are conducted to solve the problem or verify a proposed hypothesis through the collection of measurements and observations.

experimental plan A uniform and systematic way of testing the hypothesis. Experimental planning begins with correlating variables and a uniform control group.

flow chart A diagram that describes the results of a process, steps, or sequence through the use of various geometric shapes from beginning to end.

frequency distribution A mathematical summary of a set of data that shows the numerical frequency of each class of items.

histogram A graph that represents a frequency distribution. The item classes are placed along the horizontal axis and the frequencies along the vertical axis. Rectangles are drawn with the item class as the base and the frequency as the side.

hypothesis A prediction of the outcome of an experiment, or an estimated solution to the problem or question proposed in a science project.

independent variable The aspect of the experiment that is being controlled, changed, or manipulated.

Institutional Review Board (IRB) A group of science fair officials responsible for reviewing projects that involve human subjects to evaluate the possibility of physical or psychological risk.

Intel International Science and Engineering Fair (Intel ISEF) Since 1949, this science fair administered by Science Service has been held for the top science fair projects from around the world. It is considered to be the "Super Bowl" of science fairs.

journal A logbook used to record information that is gathered and learned about a science project, along with notes on progress made in the project, measurements, and data results.

life sciences category (sometimes referred to as the biological sciences category) One of the two main categories recognized by most science fairs that includes science projects encompassing the fields of behavioral and social sciences, biochemistry, botany, gerontology, medicine and health, microbiology, and zoology.

line graph A graph used to summarize information from a table. It has an x (horizontal) axis and a y (vertical) axis, where points are plotted at corresponding regions.

mean The measurement of the central location of a group of data through the use of a mathematical average. The mean is denoted by the symbol $\bar{x}$.

median The middle numerical value of a group of data listed in ascending order from the lowest number to the highest.

mode The numerical value that occurs most frequently in a group of data.

percentile   The position of one value from a set of data that expresses the percentage of the other data that lie below this value. This position of a particular percentile can be calculated by dividing the desired percentile by 100 and multiplying by the number of items in the ascending data set.

physical sciences category   One of the two main categories recognized by most science fairs that includes science projects encompassing the fields of chemistry, computer science, earth and space science, engineering, environmental science, mathematics and physics.

pie chart   A graph represented by a circle that is divided into segments. The circle represents the whole amount (100 percent), and each section represents a percentage of the whole.

purpose/problem   The problem or question you are testing or seeking to solve.

qualitative analysis   A means of analysis that is based on the findings in an experiment.

quantitative analysis   A means of analysis that is based on measurements in an experiment (always involves numbers).

report   An in-depth discussion of an entire science project from start to finish, including a subject history, research, experimental plan, data, conclusions, and so on.

research   The process by which information about the topic being studied is collected to search for possible clues in the development of the purpose or objective.

science fair   An exhibition of science projects grouped into divisions and categories. Science fairs occur on local, state, regional, and international levels. (The fairs discussed in this book refer to those affiliated with the Intel International Science and Engineering Fair.)

science project   A project investigating a scientific problem or question according to the scientific method that is done by a student in grades 5 through 12 for a local, state, regional, or international science exhibition.

scientific approach   An important judging criterion that measures whether the exhibitor shows evidence of applied scientific skill or engineering development through recognizing the scope and limitation of the issue that is being studied and addressing the scope of the problem including the quality of the work, time spent securing data, and whether the exhibitor's observations support these data.

scientific method   The basic procedure behind a science project. It consists of the problem/purpose, hypothesis, research/procedure, experiment, and analysis of results or conclusion.

Scientific Review Committee (SRC)   A group of science fair officials who review information about a proposed science project such as the subject matter, research plans, and materials to determine if a project is in compliance with rules and guidelines established by the Intel International Science and Engineering Fair and local, state, and federal laws.

standard deviation   A statistical calculation that is used when measuring the variation or spread that exists within a group of data.

statistical method   A mathematical method of calculating and analyzing project data.

time line   A diagram that shows various results or measurements that have been recorded at various stages at specific times.

variable   A part of an experiment that is changed or varied. There are dependent and independent variables.

SCIENCE NOTES

INDEX